Boosting the Adolescent Underachiever

How Parents Can Change a "C" Student into an "A" Student

Boosting the Adolescent Underachiever

How Parents Can Change a "C" Student into an "A" Student

Victor Cogen, Ed.D.

PERSEUS PUBLISHING
Cambridge, Massachusetts

Library of Congress Cataloging-in-Publication Data

Cogen, Victor.
Boosting the adolescent underachiever how parents can change a "C" student into an "A" student / Victor Cogen.
p. cm.
Includes bibliographical references and index.
ISBN 0-306-44328-7
1. Underachievers--Education. 2. Learning disabled teenagers--Education. 3. Education--Parent participation. I. Title.
LC4661.C566 1992
371.9--dc20 92-18714
CIP

ISBN 0-7382-0618-0
http://www.perseuspublishing.com

Published by Perseus Publishing
A Member of the Perseus Books Group

Printed in the United States of America

10 9 8 7 6 5 4 3 2 1

Introduction

Trying Everything

The following story is repeated by countless parents throughout the school year and even during summer vacation. A distraught parent seeks help to improve the scholastic performance of her child. Most common sense advice contains elements that, in the proper combination and setting, will produce limited results with some kids. Trudi Richards, a marketing expert and mother of an adolescent underachiever, feels she's heard and possibly tried all the suggestions available.

TRUDI: I was told he was spoiled, so I set about to unspoil him.

WRITER: How did you try to do that?

TRUDI: I discussed responsibility with him. I showed him that his father and I both had responsibilities that were obligatory. Some we didn't mind at all and some we weren't too happy about, but, nevertheless, we had to face them. Some tasks, which may not be fun, just have to be done. As an adult, you must do them. That's the way life is.

WRITER: How did he respond?

TRUDI: He said he understood.

WRITER: You then discussed his responsibilities?

TRUDI: Yes. There were some chores at home he had to do. Furthermore, he had to complete them at certain times, not when he felt like it. But I stressed that his major work was in school. That was equivalent in terms of responsibility to the jobs his father and I had.

WRITER: His response?

TRUDI: He agreed.

WRITER: Did it work?

TRUDI: I thought it did for a few days. He seemed to be taking his homework seriously. But then he came home with a C on a social studies test and a C on a geometry test.

WRITER: You feel he can do better?

TRUDI: His I.Q. is between the superior and very superior level. C work makes him an underachiever. Right?

WRITER: Yes, if he's consistently below his ability level and there isn't some other explanation for it, then he's an underachiever.

TRUDI: I heard your definition. He's an underachiever.

WRITER: What else did you do?

TRUDI: Talked to him some more.

WRITER: Lectured?

TRUDI: I suppose so. No results.

WRITER: Then?

TRUDI: I laid down the law. I let him know I had the full support of his father. He was . . .

WRITER: Where was his father during these "lectures"?

TRUDI: He's been very busy, but we've discussed Brad's situation often.

WRITER: Brad is fifteen?

TRUDI: Yes.

WRITER: Now halfway through tenth grade.

TRUDI: I see what you're hinting. Brad's been falling down on his school work for about a year and a half, but his father is still only in the background.

WRITER: Just noting the point. It may mean little.

TRUDI: Well, anyhow, I formed a set of rules just as the "experts" recommended. I have a list right here. From a specific date and thereafter Brad was to do his homework at a set time each evening or before. If he wanted to watch a special program on TV, he had to start his homework earlier and complete it before the program.

If he wanted to, he could do his assignment right after school. Notice, I took flexibility into account. He has a designated place to work and that's where he must keep his school things. He can't have any distractions while he's working, such as a radio or stereo playing. We also had a set time for him to work on the weekends.

WRITER: I assume it didn't work very well?

TRUDI: No. I didn't see any improvement. He would act as if he had finished everything. He was, he said, thoroughly prepared for the next day.

WRITER: Which was not reflected in his grades. What else did you try?

TRUDI: I offered to discuss his school work with him frequently, but he almost always said that everything was fine. I started to visit the school whenever there was an opportunity, but high school is different from elementary. It wasn't the same.

WRITER: I would hope so.

TRUDI: I was told to show a lot of interest in his work and so I did, but I don't remember all that stuff Brad is studying. Even if I did, it wouldn't matter. Brad didn't want to discuss it with me.

WRITER: What was your next step?

TRUDI: A tutor.

WRITER: Did that help?

TRUDI: Brad seemed to do better for a while, but his grades began to fall again. Besides, he needed more than one tutor. It was just too expensive.

WRITER: Then?

TRUDI: A psychotherapist. He told us that there was a deep-seated emotional involvement that arrested Brad's efforts. Some underachievers, he said, use their inadequate performance as a way of maintaining a relationship with their parents.

These particular adolescents feel that if they do well, their parents will lose interest and ignore them. By doing less than they're able to, they maintain the parental connection they desire. Their behavior becomes a habit that provides some subconscious satisfaction.

Is this so?

WRITER: There is probably an element of validity to it in some kids. You may also add that, in a few cases, underachievement and other unsatisfactory behavior is a way of getting at parents for something the kids don't like. In either case, to arrive at this type of cause may require Freudian analysis.

My position is that, for the vast majority of underachievers, the reasons are elsewhere and hardly so esoteric. School, for many of them, is boring. The environment offers more interesting activities outside of school.

Some others are having the problems of adolescence, but these problems extend beyond physiological and even social changes. They include mental and emotional development and a confusion that impinges on the social aspects of their lives as well as their studies.

TRUDI: That sounds like an answer from a book.

WRITER: It is. Mine. What else did you do?

TRUDI: Following advice, I started an incentive program. I cut off Brad's allowance but permitted him to be rewarded financially for good marks on his tests and gave him bonuses for good report card grades. He wanted to argue about it but I wouldn't listen. That's the way it had to be, I explained. If he wanted money, he had to do better in school.

But, you know, he seemed to be so unhappy and still wasn't doing better. When a friend of mine said that I was only bribing him to work, I dropped the effort. Why are you laughing?

WRITER: It could be considered a bribe, but so is a paycheck. I consider a bribe a way of getting a person to do something illegal or immoral. That hardly applies to schoolwork. A reward system has merit, but your error was not your plan but refusing to listen to your son's arguments.

TRUDI: He was claiming it was unfair.

WRITER: Maybe it was. What did you try next?

TRUDI: Punishment.

WRITER: In limited doses that works sometimes, but it hardly gets to the root of the problem. It loses its effectiveness if imposed too long. Anything else?

TRUDI: Sleepless nights.

WRITER: Yours, I suppose. How did that affect Brad?

TRUDI: I can't really say.

WRITER: I can. Now let me use some classic psychiatry. You wanted him to feel sorry for you. You might have saddled him with some guilt, but I doubt if that would have encouraged him to work harder in school.

You might go back to that psychotherapist again. This time for yourself.

TRUDI: That's what kids can do to parents. Now, what can *you* offer?

Observation

Despite, or maybe because of, my training as a curriculum specialist, educational therapist, and researcher, I have become an eclectic pragmatist. Although I lean heavily toward cognitive theory, I feel free to depart from any psychological notions of learning and behavior and to utilize and recommend whatever methodology brings favorable results. Some educators will find my approach worthy of study and expansion, but a few, I expect, will consider my unconventional approaches controversial. Ask them, if the occasion arises, *why* your child is an underachiever and what *they* are going to do about it.

The balance of this work answers the final question posed by Trudi Richards.

A Technicality

I use "he" and "she" interchangeably throughout the text while I wait for the linguists to find a suitable substitute for the awkward "he/she" or "his/her" constructions, which disrupt the flow of the text.

Acknowledgments

I am grateful to the many parents and educators who have cooperated with my efforts over the years and to those special contributors to my program, the adolescents themselves. My special thanks to teenagers Robert Willows, John T. Walters, Michele Lynne Mosley, and Regina Boyko for shedding considerable light on the current thinking of teenagers. I'm indebted also to Naomi Brier, my editor, for stressing clarity and precision and to Linda Greenspan Regan, Senior Editor, who was involved from the beginning. Finally, I dedicate this book to my wife, Betty Mosley Cogen, whose own educational administrative experience served as a continuous and vital resource.

Contents

1

Setting the Scene

In the United States, there are well over forty million students enrolled in over one hundred thousand schools. This work deals with only one student and one school—your youngster and the school he attends. The goal of this effort is to help you, as a parent, improve the scholastic performance of your underachieving teenage child.

The techniques suggested eschew almost all of the usual recommendations that you have probably tried, ranging from rewards, punishment, tutors, and learning centers, to high technology, tests, and psychotherapists. In their place is a unique program based on a new understanding of the adolescent that focuses on the underlying causes of underachievement.

This book is designed for intelligent, interested parents (or one parent) and their youngster, ages eleven to fifteen, who has been classified by the *parent* as an underachiever.

You know whether you qualify as an intelligent and interested parent, and you also know the age of your child. But what is an underachiever? For our purposes, an underachiever is a student whose scholastic performance falls *significantly* below his innate potential, and who is unhampered by anatomical, sensory, or neurological impairments, or an inner-city disadvantage. In plain language, an underachiever is a normal kid who just doesn't get the grades he should.

Jean Piaget, the late Swiss biopsychologist, whose theories reshaped the field of child development, opened the door to a new perspective on the adolescent. According to Piaget, a youngster, starting at age twelve, reaches a state designated as "formal operations," which dramatically rearranges the structure of his thinking. Understanding the significance of this change, coupled with the current recognition of the extraordinary role of emotion in learning, provides the basis for this new approach to helping the underachiever. Both of these concepts are irrevocably tied to this educational prescription and contribute to an updated and more realistic view of adolescent behavior. The result is an opportunity for parents to stimulate their child's interest in learning and boost his productive capacity.

The suggested program combines some well-established practices with a considerable number of innovative systems that may be just the right tonic for your child. The results of these techniques will depend on the individual child and, of course, on how well the parent implements them. The prediction of human behavior is more than an inexact science; it is often haphazard. The program, however, increases the chances for a happy outcome. Compare this effort, for instance, to a safe or defensive automobile driver. Such a person has improved the odds of avoiding an accident, but the possibility of a collision is not beyond question. Outside factors always intrude upon every human effort. However, the parent who chooses to follow this program raises the likelihood that her child will overcome his educational difficulties.

A typical situation involving an underachieving child is similar to the one confronting Bob's mother and father. Bob was a fourteen-year-old who had nearly everything going for him: (1) a good home in a middle-class environment, (2) intelligent and hard-working parents, (3) clear-cut family values, (4) good role models in the household, (5) no serious physical or mental health problems, and (6) superior intelligence. Despite these advantages, Bob was, without a doubt, an underachiever. Bob's parents sought advice wherever it could be found. Family members and friends offered opinions. Teachers, a counselor, and a psychologist also provided input.

The explanations for Bob's lack of acceptable progress varied. But each reason was either too general, too pat, or lacked a substantive foundation. Even in combination, the views were hardly more than speculation:

- It's just a passing phase. He'll get over it and do better.
- It's the result of peer pressure. He has the wrong friends.
- He's just lazy. The right punishment will get him moving in the right direction.
- It's in his genes, from the in-laws' side. Look at Bob's Uncle Louie.
- It's the fault of the schools. The teachers, the supervisors, and the administrators are all inept.
- That's the way adolescents are. Nothing can be done about it.
- It's your fault (you, the parent). You must have done something wrong.

If your "Bob" has failed to reach an appropriate level of achievement, it's probably not due to the causes mentioned above. You, the parent, are probably not at all culpable. On the other hand, if you do nothing to alleviate the situation, then perhaps you may rightly earn some measure of guilt. You must assume some responsibility for helping your child elevate his academic accomplishments by setting some generalized but realistic objectives and then employing the necessary techniques to reach them.

Programmatic Goals

The goals enumerated below are based on years of hands-on experience with adolescents, direct research, sound psychological theory, and updated information. Most importantly, the goals are reasonable. Implementing this program will help your child:

1. Improve his school grades through motivation and the development of a systematic approach to learning.
2. Understand the importance of learning throughout his life.
3. Gain an understanding of himself, his talents, and his abilities.
4. Build self-confidence in academic, social, and economic areas.
5. Learn to utilize his training and skills in a variety of endeavors.
6. Appreciate the importance of understanding and relating to others.
7. Develop flexibility and adjust to change as it occurs.
8. Rebound after setbacks, establish revised objectives, and pursue them vigorously.
9. Recognize problems in their early stages and plan to resolve them.
10. Comprehend the necessity for delayed gratification for the long-term good.
11. Become aware of the consequences of his actions.
12. Establish an appropriate, close, and lasting relationship with his parents.

By following the material in the subsequent chapters, you will be able to make a valuable overall assessment of your own child. You will be able to develop a profile that will serve as a basis for his personal remedial plan. You will jump the hurdle of classic views on teenagers, which distort your youngster's and your own perceptions and expectations, and apply the new data to assist in your child's educational development.

Once you have overcome the stereotypical view of teenagers and systematized your knowledge of your child, you will be able to implement a different kind of learning readiness that is applicable to adolescents. You will add the *affect*—the mental processes that include emotion, feelings, mood, and temperament—into the learning equation. You will polish your youngster's developing adult-type *cognition*, which includes concepts such as drawing inferences, generalizing, comprehending metaphors, thinking abstractly, understanding ideologies, and thinking about thinking.

The new social and psychological positions relative to adolescence, presented in lay terms, are easy to follow. You will learn how to engage the procedures described to ultimately energize the scholastic performance of your child.

Wrap-Up

To succeed in this endeavor, parents must overcome classical thinking about adolescents and consider the characteristics of their own child. General descriptions of teenagers are useful for comparisons but should not form the basis of individual decisions.

Parents must also set aside memories of their own adolescence—a difficult challenge. One school of psychology believes that teenage memories, especially those involving anxiety, are repressed. Although I don't subscribe completely to this possibility, I'm certain that traumatic memories may often be distorted.

- Memories are not of objects, people, or events but rather a reflection of how a person perceived them.
- Perceptions are under the influence of a person's emotions at the time.
- Memories with strong emotional ties to one another may become blended, thus interfering with the accuracy of recall.
- Memories may be incomplete; important details may be missing.
- Wishful thinking and a need for justification may intrude upon the truth of a memory.

Some recollections are probably very accurate, but the parent should base her approach on a program designed for her child, not for herself.

Adolescents may be underachievers for any number of reasons, but parents may never have considered the underlying, real causes. Among these are the rapid mental changes, divergent thinking, and personality inclinations of many teenagers.

The program offered is designed to build both the cognitive (thinking) and affective (emotional) infrastructure in the young person that should result in efficient, ongoing learning behavior throughout life.

Your role as a parent is not to usurp the teacher's position in school but to utilize the adolescent's natural predilections to help him reach his potential in educational as well as extracurricular efforts.

School systems will probably change considerably in the next twenty years, but any improvement will be of little use to your adolescent. Your child's future is at stake now.

Part of this program focuses on greater parental understanding of teenage development, which in of itself will have a positive influence on your youngster. Another segment of the program may be classified as mental gymnastics, which should help not only the underachiever but the family as a whole and each of its members individually. Your starting point, however, is to determine whether your child is, in fact, an academic underachiever.

2

Assessing Your Teenager

Getting Started

School districts must evaluate thousands of students. If you, a parent, have an underachieving adolescent, you have to evaluate only one. The district has the advantage of scholastic records, skilled observers, and a variety of objective tests. You have the advantage of knowing your child better, longer, and in more varied situations. You have a total familiarity with his history, and, of prime importance, you are motivated more than any teacher, counselor, or psychometrician could ever be. Given these facts, whom—the professionals or yourself—should you believe and rely on?

The answer is not at all complex. Simply use all of the data available to you from all reasonable sources and, if you're intellectually honest, you'll arrive at a very realistic and useful conclusion. To many, the task may seem frightening at first, but it is hardly overwhelming. If the school says your child is an underachiever or if you believe him to be one, then the answer is to take remedial steps to correct the situation.

Remedial measures that may raise your child's scholastic level substantially are available to you, virtually cost free. Your initial step, before implementing these measures, is to perform a parental evaluation that will help you avoid errors and set realistic goals.

Tests Shed Light

A viable appraisal of your child depends upon the answers to these two fundamental questions: How is he doing in school now and what is he capable of doing? His performance is a matter of record. His grades, allowing for occasional teacher judgmental error, reflect the quality level of his work. His innate capacity to do academic work, however, requires more investigation. Schools are not likely to solicit your opinion about your child's capability. They will, more likely, tell you their opinion. They rely partly on their subjective views, as do you, but they also make use of objective measuring instruments. These devices provide extremely valuable information about students, which helps not only in grading but in diagnosing weaknesses and placing learners into suitable situations.

Tests, administered and interpreted by skilled professionals, can shed considerable light on a student's achievements and potential. Tests elicit information about the current learning accomplishments of students in most fields, such as oral reading, reading comprehension, and reading speed. Tests measure vocabulary, computational levels, problem-solving abilities, and knowledge of literature, history, geography, biology, chemistry, and physics. Tests can reveal, in some objective way, the learner's mastery of a particular subject.

Tests can also measure skill levels such as manual dexterity and mechanical aptitude; special talents, such as music, and interests, such as sociology or engineering, can be discovered. Other tests may detect either a deprivation in vision, hearing, and motor coordination or personality impairments. Tests yield information relative to comparative intellectual levels, such as the well-known, frequently discussed, and needlessly controversial I.Q. score.

Marking by teachers frequently relies heavily on teacher-made tests that are designed to evaluate the student's achievement in a specific subject at a given time. Schools also use standardized tests, constructed by professionals. These instruments are developed with great care and tried out and modified over a period of years. All accepted I.Q. tests, for example, are of this type. School districts have a multitude of time-proven examinations available to them to help determine the success of instruction and the needs of children.

Verdict: Underachiever

Mary Ellen knew her husband was losing patience. She was attempting to describe her meeting with Junior's counselor and felt that all the facts available were important in decision making.

"Okay," John interrupted. "Junior's teachers report him either unprepared or inadequately prepared. We know that. He always says he does his homework in school."

Mary Ellen notices how John's lower jaw is jutting out, which happens whenever he is pondering anything deeply and immediately before he expresses a view. He continued, "Well, we know, and we always knew, his work is slipshod or not complete. We always knew, or at least I did, that it would catch up with him."

"I knew it, too," Mary Ellen corrects. "There were many times . . ."

"Yeah, yeah," John interrupts. "Let's not go off on tangents."

Now, she anticipates, he is going to ask for the bottom line.

"So he doesn't do well in geometry and some of his other subjects. Let's get away from the trivial details. So you had this long discussion. So what is the bottom line?"

"He should be doing better scholastically," she says dryly.

"That's it? That's what the counselor had to offer? He's an underachiever, right? That's all you found out? We didn't need a counselor to tell us that."

If this were a cartoon, Mary Ellen reflects, she could bash him over the head with the imitation Ming vase on the table behind him.

"There were other points, important ones. The counselor made some helpful-sounding suggestions. He said we needed other information before we know if Junior is an underachiever."

"Yeah, 'helpful sounding.' Some Mr. Goodwrench. The kid is an underachiever, plain and simple. Look, you don't need gobs of information. You look at the results of his ability tests, I.Q.'s and such. You compare that with his report card grades and you've got it: average I.Q., average work, above-average I.Q., above-average work. And so on. Junior is working below his level, so he's an underachiever. That's his disability. The big question is, what do we do about it?"

This impatient father represents many thousands of parents who want a clear diagnosis followed by a quick and easy solution. But human learning defies simple explanations and solutions. Underachievement, for instance, is not a disability or even a clearly defined category. It is merely a description. The equation "I.Q. = Performance" is delusive and often out of balance for certain individuals. In very large numbers of scores—thousands, averaged out—there is a reasonably high correlation between grades and intelligence scores. But even in these cases, the equilibrium may be distorted. Other facts impinge significantly on performance results.

Mary Ellen's husband is correct in identifying the key question—what can be done about a youngster's underperformance? However, he is wrong, along with many others, in reducing the essentials to overly simplified terms; that is, compare the I.Q. score and grades and you've identified the problem. Narrowly constructed assumptions, such as this one, underlying basic principles make weak girders. A true picture requires more understanding of both intelligent quotients and teacher grades.

What is an I.Q. number and why do lay people and professionals alike place so much reliance and trust in it? What does it really portray and how accurate is that portrayal? I.Q.'s have been written about and discussed ad nauseam, but there is still no means, not even with an I.Q. test, to determine underachievement unless some estimate of innate ability exists. A brief review of the I.Q. is necessary to grasp the true meaning of diagnosing underachievement.

The other side of the equation is marks. Do grades really reflect a student's performance and, if so, how well? Are teachers adequately trained in grading and in developing the tests they rely on? Does the student in question know how to prepare for and take these tests? Has he really been evaluated accurately?

Grades reflect the opinion of individual teachers who combine the results of the examinations they have administered with other indications of learning, such as class performance, homework, papers, and projects. Part of the assessment is subjective, but teachers learn to combine the measuring elements into a system that yields creditable results.

Standardized tests, employed frequently, measure knowledge and/or ability levels for the purpose of comparing the performance of individual students with large groups. These devices are usually developed by states, universities, or private test-making organizations. The tests are a worthwhile measure of the student's achievement in particular subjects. When standardized tests are combined with individual grades as determined by teachers, the school and the parent have a fairly reliable measure of the child's performance level.

Therefore, on the surface, Mary Ellen's husband has the right idea. Look at the kid's potential as indicated by the tests and compare his possibilities with his actual level of work. *The error, however, is assuming that the comparison, while good for evaluating the many, is satisfactory for the individual.* The comparison in and of itself is not incorrect; it is, rather, incomplete. Parents should make a much more comprehensive evaluation before arriving at a conclusion about their child's performance.

I.Q.'s

You may, if you wish, ignite a controversy at a dull party by presenting a dogmatic stand on the validity of intelligence quotients. Even those who have never analyzed or administered such a test tend to hold strong opinions about these scores. Parents whose children have high I.Q.'s feel that the test reasonably reflects a child's native ability and that its use is justified. Others are not so sure and have misgivings about relying on a test score for judging their children. In this book both groups are considered correct. This apparent incongruity stems from the observation that the I.Q. test does adequately measure what it purports to measure, but, at the same time, it omits aspects of intelligence not yet clarified.

Note that psychologists have produced, and continue to produce, papers, articles, and books on the subject in heavy volume. They are as fascinated with intelligence tests as historians are with the Civil War and are just as prolific.

The purpose here is to avoid a scholarly in-depth analysis, but to extract the essentials necessary to help you help your underachiever. To assess your child's potential, you should peruse these brief statements about I.Q. tests.

- Intelligence tests measure many of the attributes necessary for mastering school-type work.
- They measure aspects of intelligence such as general perception, perceptual motor coordination, logical reasoning, short-term memory, long-term memory, and verbal ability. (Opinions differ as to the number and specificity of primary mental abilities that actually exist, their relationship to one another, and their linkage to general, overall intellectual functions.)
- I.Q. tests are an acceptable estimate of your child's scholastic potential. They are developed meticulously and tested and modified repeatedly before being marketed.
- They are less accurate in predicting the postschool success of individuals in the "real world." After school, many other factors enter the picture.

- I.Q. tests, consisting of a score or two that attempts to describe a child's complete intellectual capacity, could lead one astray. There are numerous aspects of intelligence, including some that have yet to be clearly identified. Reduced to one score, the I.Q. represents only an average of various types of abilities measured by the test.
- I.Q. tests are not accepted by all professionals. Some of the world's leading researchers dispute the efficacy of these tests as currently designed. Jean Piaget said, "I have no faith in measures that are based on intelligence quotients or any other performance measure."
- They are not very helpful in measuring the emotional component involved in learning and in performance.
- They are rather consistent in their results. Although scores of a particular child change from test to test and over time, they tend to remain in the same general range. A child whose average I.Q. scores in elementary school were about 100 is not likely to raise his average to 140 by high school. Parents should pay little attention to the exact score but should look at the general level of the youngster to determine his academic potential. Performance expectations usually look something like the following:

90–109	Average
110–119	Above average
120–129	Superior
130–up	Very superior

- I.Q. tests seem not to be influenced by gender in overall intellectual ability.
- Detractors of I.Q. tests say they contain a built-in cultural bias. Test makers have endeavored to eliminate such a bias over many years. This factor, if it exists, is not related to underachievement as defined here.
- I.Q. tests tend to influence people in and out of education and psychology and can alter expectations of teachers.
- For schools they are, in fact, a useful measure to understand and place children in appropriate learning settings. Many

other tests reveal helpful information about a student. The I.Q. tests, as the others, have their limitations, and parents should collect additional information whenever possible.

Intelligence tests fail to adequately measure the child's creative potential, which is an extremely important element of human capability. The level of creativity, society's key to progress, may affect the personality of the child. A highly creative child, thwarted in his urge to produce a nonstandard product, may lose interest in school and become an underachiever.

Some psychologists believe that intelligence in adolescents, which is our focus, becomes more and more differentiated than the global type observed in younger children. Not all researchers follow Piaget's notion of a new stage in the developmental process, but view mental growth as a continuum. As far as parents are concerned, whatever the process and the theory to explain the teenager's new thinking systems, they are significant since they affect his learning ability and behavior.

Some fields of endeavor require a high level of intellectual capability similar to the ones measured by intelligence tests. One of these, for instance, is astronomy (mentioned by teenagers rather frequently in recent years as a favorite area of interest), in which the ability to comprehend the most complex theories in physics and master the most sophisticated mathematical procedures is essential. Anyone with an average or just above average I.Q. might be well advised to relegate this interest to a hobby and opt for a less intellectually demanding pursuit, such as politics.

The I.Q. score standing by itself has value and, for certain purposes, should not be disregarded. A battery of tests performed by a competent psychometrician—an individual who engages in the administration of mental tests—is, of course, far more useful. The schools, with a student's cumulative record and the results of various tests, make judgments and recommendations about each student. Parents should incorporate these judgments and recommendations into a total assessment program. Remember—they're useful but just one part of the whole.

Parental Evaluation

The most obvious place to begin is with the aforementioned evaluation performed by the school, which is most likely sufficient and accurate for the purposes of the school. Your needs may be considerably different. You want as many test results as the educational system can provide, but not in terms of raw scores. Teachers and counselors will be able to interpret scores in terms of what is being measured and how the results compare to your child's age group nationally. The results may be somewhat different than a comparison with his class or the student body of the school he attends. Standardized test score levels are based on the population, by age or grade, coast to coast, thus providing you with a broad picture of your child's skills and achievement.

The staff at the school will also provide you with an enhanced report on your child's achievement and some personal views, usually quite valuable, explaining what your child should be doing and, perhaps, offering some insight into why he isn't doing it. Some worthwhile remedial suggestions might also be included. You'll probably leave with helpful information not generally found on a "report" card. If you visit as a cooperative parent, quite willing to listen intently (note taking is quite acceptable), and ask pertinent questions, you will be successful in getting the information you need for your own remedial program.

Some schools may avoid providing you with all the information available, which is another of those controversial positions. Don't worry. You don't need absolutely everything, because your aim isn't precision. At this stage, you're just trying to establish a range of ability and performance and perhaps discover some strategies that might fit into your developing plan. Be careful not to play the role of an expert, even if you are. You are on an information search, not a witch hunt. With the school's information, you will have a greater knowledge of your child's potential skill in academics and perhaps understand a bit more about the work he actually does.

You don't have to know the exact scores of all the tests. For instance, on your child's latest intelligence test result you are adequately informed if you have his approximate position on the hierarchy: average, above average, superior, or very superior. That is sufficient for your purposes. The test makers themselves usually allow a five-point plus-or-minus margin of error.

If you know a high percentage of what the school knows, you are better informed than they because you have and will collect additional data. Furthermore, you will be considering additional factors that are inadequately covered by intelligence and aptitude tests.

Wrap-Up

Get as much information as possible from your child's school, including test results, teachers' views, and counselor's opinions.

Consider the information provided by the school as one segment of a picture of your child. Every test score and every professional observation is important, but none of them, standing alone, should dictate your evaluative results.

You can't avoid the influence of the I.Q., but that, too, should not be accepted in isolation when developing a scholastic remedial program. Other pieces of information must be factored in as well. As a parent, you are already familiar with many aspects of your child's personality and ability. An effective way to start is to organize the knowledge you already have by creating a profile of your youngster.

3

Creating an Informal Profile

As a parent, you are in a unique position to assemble a psychological profile of your teenager. Before your friendly maven tells you to back off because you're not properly trained for this, read on. The profile I suggest is obtainable by reasonably intelligent adults who have no special training in psychology, education, sociology, or nuclear physics. The less you know about Pavlov's dogs, Harlow's primates, Skinner's pigeons, Freud's analyses, Allport's social encounters, and Chomsky's syntactical structures, the more qualified you are to perform the task ahead. The more you know about classical approaches, the more you will try to make your observations fit professional molds instead of using the prescription proffered. Psychologists refer to this phenomenon as *proactive inhibition,* or the interference of earlier learning on later study.

Let's look at what you have so far. You are in possession of or can obtain necessary information about your child from the school. As a parent, you have additional knowledge. Now, you're going to combine the data from the school with the observations and memories floating around in your mental computer. Your goal is to combine your understandings with the information from the school and arrange the elements to produce an enlightening picture.

You will be told you are biased in your judgments, and so you may be. Parents do, at times, exaggerate the potential and accomplishments of their children or make excuses for weaknesses, but this is an in-house evaluation. The exercise is for you alone, not for the critics. You're going to be more objective than you think since you need not share the profile with anyone. The privacy of this exercise obviates the urge to impress others, leaving, instead, the inclination to do a good and effectual analysis.

Sit back and reflect on each item that appears on the form that follows.* You may do this as a husband and wife team, with another person who knows and loves your child, or by yourself. Have no concern over phraseology or spelling, punctuation or literary merit. If you're not sure of commas and semicolons use dashes. No one is going to grade your effort. The only gold star you will earn is in your imagination. You are merely making notes to yourself, and if you can't think of the precise word to express a thought, put anything down. You can change it later, or not, as determined by you. You're putting what you know about your child on paper in order to organize your thoughts and perceptions.

You might not be sure of what to write, or you may feel that you lack insight into some category. Remember that this isn't supposed to be a comprehensive instrument. If in doubt, leave a space blank. You will certainly have enough information to form a fresh slant on your child that will help in formulating a remedial program to raise his academic level and work performance for life.

Finally, you may find that some of your views are deeply submerged in your subconscious. They may arise when you are doing something else or in the middle of the night. You will want to allow the profile to "age" for a few days to allow for additional thoughts and revisions.

The list of evaluative items below is designed to help a parent assess her child as required by the plan in this work. Although some professionals may disagree, the meanings provided are adequate to meet the purposes of this assessment.

* You may find it convenient to photocopy the profile form.

Scholars spend years (yes, years) debating word definitions, sometimes without resolution. For instance, the first item, personality, has the same or nearly the same connotation for the majority of laypersons. If you speak of one's personality, most listeners will grasp the context in which you use the word and derive an adequate understanding. Freud, Adler, Allport, Jung, Cattell, and others, however, had their unique versions of "personality." Your task is to avoid preoccupation with all of the possibilities indicated by a term and continue with the program. My definitions will do quite nicely for this exercise. Where I don't think you can go wrong, I don't provide a definition, only a comment.

By committing your thoughts about your child to paper, you automatically modify the data. Thinking undergoes revision when written. The process of writing forces you to complete a thought that may only be dangling in its mental structures. You also notice, and therefore discount, redundancies. You force yourself to clarify nebulous observations and fill in important gaps that you didn't realize were there. While thinking, your mind may wander and cause you to stray from your objective. Writing forces you to focus on the subject at hand, and since this issue is so vital, you will be motivated to finish your own assignment.

Some parents still resist, initially, filling out a form. As one said, "Couldn't I just talk and record my thoughts on a tape?" She was unhappy with my answer, which wasn't a "No." "Record if you're comfortable with that format, but then write it down as directed." Writing will not only clarify your thoughts, but it will highlight areas of weakness.

In addition to the reasons mentioned, add two others. The process of creating a parental assessment of your child requires comparing items, that is, how they interrelate, and interrelationships are easier to pick out if the items are actually there in front of you. It may be faster to think, and faster to talk, but it's more effective to write. Second, you now have a readily accessible record for a later review of your present thinking. At some future date, you may find it extremely useful to return to your original assessment for a comparison with your later revised opinions, as well as to note any progress in your child.

Parental Educational Analysis Profile

Personality

Describe the totality of your child's unique emotional and behavioral traits, especially as they are perceived by you.

Maturity

Does your child act his age?

Peer Popularity

The degree of acceptance of your child by teenagers of his own age and his own sense of belonging to this group.

Sibling Relationship

The ability to get along with, help, seek help from, and live in reasonable harmony with his sisters and brothers.

Parental Relationship

How well does your child relate to you on an average over time? First write down your immediate impressions; then, after completing the chapter on adolescent characteristics, return to this item and modify it as necessary.

General Health

Unless there is some specific problem that interferes with his general well-being and/or performance (e.g., asthma), mark your child in terms of satisfactory or better than average health. Teenagers are, on the whole, a healthy lot, and we have already eliminated those who suffer from sensory, emotional, and intellectual handicaps.

Energy Level

Rate this with a word or two such as "normal" or "below average," based on a comparison with other children his age.

Sleep Habits

Adolescents should sleep well most of the time. If your child does not or sleeps too much, consider a thorough medical checkup.

Activities

List as many as you can and the extent of his interest. Include such items as athletics, hobbies, "hanging out" with the gang, clubs (younger adolescents), dates by couples or in groups, dances, school, church and sponsored entertainment, movies, trips, after-school projects, and jobs.

Special Interests

These may duplicate one or more of the above, but he indicates a preference for them and spends a disproportionate amount of time engaging in them whenever he can.

Persistence

On the positive side, this is the resolute pursuing of task completion. The negative side is a stubborn clinging to a position in spite of evidence to the contrary.

Temper

Disregard all meanings except for an evaluation of how quickly he departs from a normal calm and becomes angry or, worse, loses control.

Emotional Reaction

List the aspects of living that he responds to and easily shows emotion toward, such as happiness, the extension of love, appreciation or disdain, scorn, and rejection. Consider laughter or crying to be emotional reactions.

Sense of Humor

The ability to perceive something amusing or clever in a situation or character. Incongruities and peculiarities may become foils for his wit.

Self-Perception

The private image he has of himself in all-important aspects of living, which may not necessarily be what he says it is. Parents can frequently detect this view better than others.

Confidence Level

His own level of certitude about himself when faced with a difficult task.

General Motivation

How well he is inclined to follow various pursuits and the type of inducement necessary for him to act.

Attitude toward School

As an underachiever, he may be expected to dislike or merely tolerate school. However, some underachieving adolescents like school, not for the academics but for the other activities.

Overall School Performance

Irrespective of grades, how much off the mark you think he actually is. Does he do well in subjects he likes? Does he improve when prodded by you? Does he accept or resist scholastic challenges?

Academic Track Record

The accumulation of his performance over time, including elementary school. Do not use an average, but chart the ups and downs of his performance over the years.

Strong Subjects

List individual items and the history of your child's skill in this area.

Weak Subjects

List individual weak subjects and the history of your child's performance in these areas. If he is currently weak in mathematics, for instance, was this always true?

Emerging Talents

This frequently overlooked aspect is among the most important. Consider this a combination of interest and skill development providing a strong hint as to his future possibilities in school and afterward.

Samples

The following are examples of the efforts of mothers of underachieving teenagers to analyze their own adolescents. They were selected because of some common statements. Each parent said she (1) disliked filling out forms, (2) couldn't see any particular use for the exercise, (3) was not particularly adept at writing, (4) had no training in such endeavors (i.e., analysis), and (5) was concerned about grammar or punctuation, irrespective of my directions.

This form is for you as a parent. Forget how well you express yourself and concentrate on content. You know more about your kid than you think. You can fill out the form in ten minutes or half a day, but it should, if you stop to reflect carefully about each item, consume about one hour.

I did make some corrections on the samples presented for the sake of clarity. The thoughts and the wording are strictly those of the parents. Each mother agreed to have her child's profile included in this work but without personal identification. Notice the brevity of the parental responses, which typifies the majority of profiles, but certainly not all.

Some parents attached additional sheets of paper to the form. Follow your own inclinations and write as much or as little as you desire. The sentences in parentheses are my comments.

In simple, clear language these parents reveal useful and insightful information about their children, despite their initial reluctance to write down their thoughts.

Sample A (Fifteen-year-old Girl in Tenth Grade)

Personality

Friendly, outgoing, very naive.

Maturity

Outgoing, giggly and immature, but can act her age and be very responsible at times.

Peer Popularity

Popular with boys and girls, but especially with boys.

Sibling Relationship

Very protective of her sister, but loses patience quickly.

Parental Relationship

Seems comfortable discussing just about anything with me—her father too, if he is there at the time.

General Health

Healthy (doesn't smoke, drink, or do drugs).

Energy Level

Average.

Sleep Habits

Fine.

Activities

Plays guitar. No sports. Likes to dance. Loves to hang out with the boys. Fits right in with the boys.

Special Interests

She plays her guitar for hours and then she won't pick it up for a week.

Persistence

She will listen to what her father and I have to say but will still do what she thinks is right. In the end she realizes that we were right and will admit it. Many of her friends do drugs and I've overheard them pressuring her, but she is completely against it and won't give in.

Temper

Even-tempered.

Emotional Reaction

Laughs very easily. Isn't moody. If she is, she usually tells us why. Have noticed that she has gotten more emotional with me if I hurt her feelings.

Sense of Humor

Seems to find humor in almost anything.

Self-Perception

I feel she does think she's something special, but if we try to tell her why the boys really like her, she thinks we're wrong and that they only like her for her personality.

Confidence Level

Doesn't seem to have a lot of confidence in herself when it comes to her guitar playing, but as far as appearance is concerned, she seems to have lots.

General Motivation

As far as schoolwork or something she doesn't really want to do, not too much motivation. But if it's something she wants to do, she has a lot.

Attitude toward School

Enjoys going to school, but I would say more for socializing.

Overall School Performance

When we push her she'll be a B or A student, but if we don't, she is a C or D student.

Academic Track Record

Real good up to fifth grade. Always had a problem with talking. Problems started in sixth grade. Would fail or get a D average one marking period, then we would punish her (ground her) and she would bring the grades up. She's been doing this every year.

Strong Subjects

Does okay in science and in math and can do very well if she tries hard.

Weak Subjects

Weak in social studies and English.

Emerging Talents

Seems to have a lot of talent in music. She can listen to a song a few times and then pick it up on her guitar. I feel if she gave it her all she could really do something with it.

Sample B (Fourteen-year-old Boy in Ninth Grade)

Personality

Takes himself and life much too seriously. Hesitates before he speaks on serious subjects. It's like he doesn't hear or care, but then he gives a thoughtful response.

Maturity

Has always been mature.

Peer Popularity

Boys call him, but he doesn't call them very often. He goes out with friends sometimes, but not as much as I would like.

Sibling Relationship

Normal sibling confrontations. Nothing out of the ordinary.

Parental Relationship

He doesn't question authority. But you have to have a very good reason for telling him to do this or that.

General Health

No real problems. Except for "large nose" and "zits" and "his whole life going down the toilet"! (His mother is quoting him.)

Energy Level

Above average. He has to be involved in some activity all the time.

Sleep Habits

No problem here!

Activities

Motorcycle riding (on property set up for this purpose). Has taught himself to play guitar. Loves model building—anything involving working with his hands. Hanging out.

Special Interests

Motorcycle riding, working on any kind of mechanical things.

Persistence

Above average. Compulsive to a certain extent but not as bad as his father. (The boy's father reviewed this profile and deleted the comment referring to his own compulsiveness. His mother put it back in.)

Temper

Very seldom shows temper. Never loses control.

Emotional Reaction

Pretty steady emotionally but can be a real mope at times. Sometimes he laughs at himself.

Sense of Humor

He laughs at himself but would rather laugh at someone else. He can usually see the funny side of things.

Self-Perception

I think for the most part he has a good self-image, but he likes to have this reinforced for him frequently.

Confidence Level

If the task is something he is familiar with, he has a lot of confidence. On the other hand, if it's something unfamiliar to him, he does lack confidence.

General Motivation

Little interest in school in general. His motivation is either monetary or looking good to peers.

Attitude toward School

Poor. He feels there are many more interesting aspects to life. He does enough to get by gradewise, but that's about it.

Overall School Performance

I think he can do well if he is motivated. We don't know how to achieve this—though we do try.

Academic Track Record

Not too good. He did better in early grades—then he learned he could goof off and still get by.

Strong Subjects

Any subject involving using his hands—woodworking, mechanical drawing, etc. In statewide competitions he wins prizes for his work. He does good work when he has time to think things through—can't be rushed.

Weak Subjects

Anything that smacks of literature. He says it's not real. Considers most subjects "garbage."

Emerging Talents

Mechanical reasoning. He takes pride in working out mechanical problems. He plans before he starts. He also has the ability to get along with people and to get them to see things his way.

Sample C (Thirteen-year-old Girl in Eighth Grade)

Personality

Usually outgoing.

Maturity

Always mature.

Peer Popularity

Accepted by peers. Always one of the group—both sexes.

Peer Relationship

Peacemaker in family with two brothers.

Parental Relationship

I feel she has always been close to me. Being a teenager is not changing this.

General Health

No real problems.

Energy Level

Below average. If not doing something specific, she goes to bed—like a cat.

Sleep Habits

No problem here.

Activities

Hanging out, dancing, parties, going out.

Special Interests

Loves music, reads popular magazines, into fashions, interested in lives of celebrities.

Persistence

Average or above. Never starts a project that she doesn't finish.

Temper

Even-tempered.

Emotional Reaction

Normal reactions to situations—readily laughs or cries, depending on situation.

Sense of Humor

Appreciates humor. Finds herself funny.

Self-Perception

Good self-image.

Confidence Level

When she isn't sure about capabilities she gets an "attitude." When the task has been accomplished, then she'll confide that she had doubts.

General Motivation

Depending on interest. She'll do what is necessary for self-satisfaction.

Attitude toward School

Not particularly interested. She gets decent grades because of her personal standards. She doesn't want to miss school, because she might miss what's going on. The work is secondary. (Test scores place her in the very superior level.)

Overall School Performance

Above average—could do better. She should be an A student.

Academic Track Record

She did well until she was about twelve—then dipped. Then her grades went back up. I think she discovered boys, but she denies this.

Strong Subjects

English, literature.

Weak Subjects

Math.

Emerging Talents

She shows leadership ability. If she ever decides to use all she's got, she'll be way in front of the pack.

Confidence in Your Assessment

The evaluation of your child need not be a laborious effort but, if approached as advised, a fun game. It doesn't matter if you're not a teacher, psychologist, counselor, or other expert in the field of education. Ask yourself, however, what parent among the billions on earth knows your kid better than you do? From the standpoint of parental expertise, therefore, you are in the 99th percentile (the percentage of people you surpass in a particular category). In addition, you have collected considerable information from trained observers that you will blend with your own. You should admit to some combination of bias and wishful thinking, but you're not out to elevate your child to some lofty goal out of his reach. You merely want the best for him based not on any fantasy but on his ability. Put your reluctance, if it exists, aside and think about it:

- The assessment scheme you are using is designed for parents, not professionals. Many items usually considered useful by professionals have been omitted because experience has demonstrated that they contribute little to this particular effort.
- You are not studying the discipline of either psychology or education; you are judging your child. Your purpose is not to change or even criticize the school but to simply find ways that your child may take advantage of the school's offerings.
- You have the essentials of your child's history imprinted in your memory. You have information not available to the schools, which may explain your child's lack of achievement. You know the behavioral patterns of your kid in a whole variety of settings.
- *You* are the true expert on your child.
- You are going to utilize all of the available facts about your youngster for purposes that will soon be specified. You will combine these facts, in ways not available to the school districts, to seek useful revelations. If, in so doing, you are guilty of incorporating into the mix some parental intuition, so much the better. Scientists depend on hunches and feelings; why should you be different?
- You accept the notion that your evaluation has its limitations, but you also know that the state of the art on adolescence is rather nebulous, and the professional understanding of how all people learn is both limited and controversial. You can match that. You can arrive at a nebulous, limited, and controversial conclusion.
- Your own involvement in turning your child's educational performance around is itself likely to promote a greater effort on his part. By examining the data, you are opening the door to serendipity. Something you weren't actually seeking may arise to help yield the results you desire.

As always, a caveat or two or more is in order. Avoid simplistic explanations about your child, who is as complex an individual as all other humans. Avoid overly broad impressions that seemingly apply to everything. For instance, if he doesn't do well in general, does he succeed in specific subjects? Also, avoid focusing on exceptions that may not account for his subpar performance. Perhaps he doesn't like a particular teacher and doesn't do well in her class, but that should not be the explanation for lack of performance in other classes and in earlier years. Finally, disregard fad theories that constantly arise to explain, without substance, how everything is wrong with the schools and why your Johnny can't read or learn well enough. Concentrate, instead, on assessing your teenager's ability to learn at a rate commensurate with his innate ability and on determining what his true level of ability is.

Wrap-Up

1. The purpose of your assessment is to broaden the view of your child provided by grades and tests.
2. The professional assessment of your child's potential may lack essential considerations because of (a) lack of knowledge of your child as an individual and (b) the limitations of the art of testing.
3. You are providing material that may uncover clues to your child's underachievement and suggest remedial measures to upgrade his performance.
4. You are searching for your child's unused strengths and the weaknesses that interfere with his academic progress. You are being alert to the possibility of uncovering some untested and unrecognized talent and ability.
5. You are preparing academic motivational systems based on your twelve or more years of knowing your child the way no one else does.
6. You are determining the emotional aspects of your child's learning with information unavailable to educators, such as personal interests, topic motivation, and study habits.

Comparing potential ability test results with academic success has its usefulness, but anytime your child appears to be underperforming, a closer evaluation is essential. You are providing the services of another expert to add information and take evaluative steps beyond those taken by teachers, counselors, or psychologists. You are the expert now. The work is rather interesting and the payoff is incredibly gratifying.

We shall return to this exercise in Chapter 16. The act of completing the profile at this stage, before you are influenced by the material to be described, will serve as a valuable basis of comparison with your later thinking. If you wish, you may review your assessment at any time and even modify your comments. The exercise will have already fulfilled its task, that is, to organize your thinking about the characteristics of your child. You are now ready to gain some insight into adolescents in general and how your teenager compares with others. We start in the next chapter with current and somewhat revised views of children ages twelve to sixteen.

4

Adolescent Characteristics
An Updated Review

Even Adolescents Are Individuals

Most scientists are convinced, despite widespread doubts in the past, that the laws of physics are the same everywhere in the universe. The theories about these laws may be incomplete, but when all things are equal, the results of a known event are invariant. If, in a given set of precise conditions, *x* changes into *y*, then, when those conditions are operable, *x* will change into *y*. Not sometimes; not most of the time. Always.

Your automobile has been designed to follow the rules of physics. If it doesn't start, then a change in the existing conditions has occurred. Mechanical principles have not been suspended. It's possible that your car has a malfunction in its ignition system, the battery is dead, the starter is worn, the gas tank is empty, or the temperature is too low. Your automobile cannot be capricious despite your inclinations to believe so. If it doesn't start, the conditions, in some negative way, have been altered.

Whether a given inorganic event occurs on Earth or on Mars or in another solar system, if the elements of the situation are exactly the same, the results will be the same. That's a law of the universe.

If the prevailing conditions are equal, humans may be expected to behave in a prescribed fashion. If someone in a building yells FIRE, and the unmistakable smell of smoke permeates the air, most people will seek egress, quickly and probably in panic.

However, behavioral events associated with humans can never be precisely equal, which immediately precludes the comparison with a physical experiment. Certainly, people are not equal. They may behave in a similar fashion in specified circumstances, but never, absolutely never can 100 percent conformity be guaranteed. Of the five and one-half billion people presently alive, no two are alike in all characteristics—not in appearance, not in personality, not in ability, and not in behavior.

This, of course is patently obvious, and psychologists have never expected people's responses to an occurrence to be totally predictable. Educators view the notion of individual characteristics as a given. Each student is one of a kind with his own arrangement of skills, knowledge, and ability. Each student, too, has weaknesses somewhere in his panoply of abilities. If the highs and lows of each pupil in a given grade level were charted, even though there were hundreds or even thousands of youngsters involved, no two of them would be the same—similar, but not the same. Your child is different from every other in the universe. With that as a vital but sometimes forgotten consideration, let's look at adolescent characteristics.

"How," the distraught mother questioned, "could you fail English? You're good at English. Especially literature. You like literature. How . . . ?"

Peggy stared beyond her mother's left shoulder at the landscape painting on the wall as if waiting for a plausible explanation to suddenly appear. None did. She needed, she quickly concluded, a strategy. If she didn't satisfy her mother's demand for justification of the failing grade, she'd be grounded this weekend. She couldn't afford to miss Saturday night. Ted was taking her to Cathy's party and that couldn't be passed up. She'd been waiting for an opportunity to invite Ted to something and this was it. He had accepted without hesitation and even seemed quite pleased at having been asked. She couldn't miss this.

"Mom, I really wasn't feeling well during the test. I couldn't think clearly, you know. It was just a freak. It'll never happen again."

"Weren't feeling well? Don't hand me that manure, young lady. You must have recovered quickly. Wasn't that the day you went to the mall right after school with Beth and Cathy? Sure it was. You didn't say anything about being sick."

"I was sick!" claimed the daughter with vehemence. "It must have been something I ate for lunch. By the time school was over, it passed. I felt better. So there!"

"Don't you have English in the morning?"

Peggy felt trapped as she realized the lie was making her situation worse. She needed time to find a way out of this.

"You're always picking on me. One lousy English mark. You just don't understand!" She turned and quickly climbed the stairs. Her mother stood motionless, nonplussed.

What do you do with a fifteen-year-old who doesn't seem to make sense? Peggy had been a good student in elementary school, but now she showed good effort sometimes and indifference at other times. How could she fail a test in her best subject? Why was she using such childish excuses like illness? Didn't she know why she failed?

Peggy knew. She had planned to study the week before the test, but the days just got away from her. Something important kept coming up. She postponed her studying until the final weekend. That might have been sufficient time, but Cathy and Megen stopped in to pick her up on Saturday. They were shopping bound and invited her along.

Oh, well. She could study on Sunday. She did open her material early Sunday but, faced with the full extent of the material, decided there wasn't enough time. No one could learn all of that in just a few hours. What did they want from her? Who has to know all that stuff, anyhow?

Peggy's priorities were in disarray. She had continuously postponed a task until there was insufficient time for its completion. Rather than face the cause of her failure, which she understood, she employed excuses, a tactic not unknown to many teenagers.

Looking In: The Traditional and Generally Accepted View

Teenagers are noted for wild swings in emotions, from sulking to an almost contagious joy. They may, at a given point in time, be depressed, only to escape the heavy cloud overshadowing them just one day later. The change, too, could come about in a minute. A phone call from a friend might stimulate the sudden metamorphosis.

Their sullen moods might resemble the characteristics of depression:

- Despondency
- Pessimism
- Feelings of inadequacy
- Reduced activity
- Self-imposed isolation

These temporary mood swings to the dark side are not indicative of a serious psychological disturbance. Pathological cases, for example, are generally ongoing and carried to some extreme. In mental illness, despondency and feelings of inadequacy transform into an overriding sense of hopelessness depicted by an unresponsiveness to stimuli. The degree of involvement of these feelings and their effect on general activity determine the seriousness of the situation.

The normal adolescent, from time to time, will exhibit some

scary qualities but will not sustain them for any significant length of time. One day your child may argue every point of an issue, including trivial ones, be unkind in a description of you, and withdraw to her room. The next morning, she may appear for breakfast, happy and smiling, with yesterday's events erased from history. Teenagers' moods seesaw without predictability.

Your teenager may have a short fuse, one that ignites seemingly without provocation, quickly reaches a powder keg, and explodes. She may, for instance, be particularly sensitive to criticism; a trivial remark may generate a volcanic eruption.

Many parents will express bewilderment to a spouse or another adult after a teenager overreacts.

"What did I say?"

The teen period is one of inconsistency as the behavioral pendulum swings from activity to inactivity. Teenagers may persevere in attempting to complete a homework assignment or special project or without explanation quit prematurely. The first obstacle encountered may engender an adverse reaction.

"That teacher doesn't know what she's doing. She assigns anything. Look at it. It doesn't make any sense."

"I can't do this; I can't do this kind of work. I'm just dumb."

"This isn't for me. I'll never use this again. It's just a time waster. I've got better things to do."

When a parent has convinced the youngster to plan carefully, to collect the necessary facts and materials before beginning an assignment, the battle may be won. Prepared, the learner will attack the challenge in the most efficient and logical manner, time will be saved, and the product will be of a higher quality. Sometimes.

Despite prior success with planning, the adolescent, for no explicable reason, may impulsively undertake another task. No designing. No preparation. No overview. No smooth sailing.

"The teacher doesn't know . . ."

"I can't do this . . ."

"Who needs this . . ."

The same inconsistency may apply to nonschool endeavors. A

party or trip may be carefully charted out with each aspect endlessly scrutinized, or an offhand suggestion may be followed by an impulsive "Let's do it!"

Teenagers display a tendency toward rash activity in many areas. They may decide something is desirable and become extremely impatient. They want it NOW. Parents find many adolescents to be self-indulgent, fussing over inessential items. Stores that cater to impulse buying, displaying goods attractive to teenagers, do well, provided they stay abreast of the trends.

Sometimes adolescents confound their parents by swinging in the opposite direction, away from material possessions, toward asceticism. Usually, this is tied in with topics heralded by the news media at the time, such as concern for people deprived of basics (food and shelter), or social and political rights. The teenager may be quick to adopt a cause concerning poverty in Central America, starvation in northeast Africa, and refugees throughout the world. The victims of storms, floods, and earthquakes are added as short-term concerns to the continuous plight of millions of people in distress.

The adolescent follows the news media as it shifts its focus from the homeless to the unacceptable squalor in some sections of the inner cities. Just as television seeks fresh-breaking stories to hold its audience, the teenager tires of his empathy toward people in despair and discovers new interests. A red sports car will usually distract the middle-class teenager from the cause of the have-nots. He'll retain a few choice phrases blithely uttered to cover the issue when it arises, but his concern is clearly shallow.

Teenagers may be quite argumentative at times. Their positions are usually simplistic and inculpating. If a problem exists, solve it. If money is required, get it. If construction is necessary, build it. If something is wrong, someone is to blame. "No fault" isn't part of their vocabularies.

Tina carefully explains to her parents that fossil fuels are pollutants and must be prohibited. Atomic energy is dangerous and should be discontinued. Other sources of energy—wind, geothermal, water—are, she acknowledges, limited. But, she smiles knowingly, an answer exists. She deliberately searches among her materials for her proof. "There," she exclaims triumphantly. She holds up a miniature calculator. "Solar power. No pollution! Renewable! Unlimited!"

Her mother nods in agreement. She explains patiently that solar power is an ideal solution. But, she emphasizes, solar technology is still inadequate to power heavy vehicles or factories or to provide the energy that electric companies must distribute.

"That's just it. You people, your generation has nothing but excuses. You're guilty of negligence." The accused, both parents, look at each other and shrug. They don't appreciate it, but their daughter has a large armamentarium of criticism ready to hurl in their direction.

Addressing the adolescent, the mother requests, "Dear, turn out the light in the dining room, please." The youngster, unmindful of her parent's request, walks past the switch and ignores it.

Teen interaction with peers is intense and reciprocal. Alexander Graham Bell's "intriguing toy" has become an unending instrument of satisfaction to youngsters. After returning from school with their friends or engaging in some kind of game with their friends or meeting with their friends or cruising a mall with their friends or attending a movie with their friends or getting a hamburger with their friends, they return home and, of course, immediately call their friends.

The conversations never cease; the reservoir of subjects is inexhaustible. Many have or want their own phones, and technology is advancing their cause. Telephones in cars are becoming more common and portable telephones are already popular. Soon, some parents predict, every teenager will have a telephone hooked to or growing out of his hip. As a beneficial side effect, parents will be able to dial their offspring with important messages such as "It's ten o'clock. Get home right away."

Of equal importance to the telephone are automobiles, clothes, and hair styles. Adolescents yearn for the day they can become licensed drivers and even car owners. The latter goal is frequently frustrated by the high cost of insurance, which many parents, unjustly of course, demand the adolescent pay for.

Adolescents may avoid being seen with parents in public places. Family visits may be described as boring. They prefer being with friends and being seen with friends. Being seen with parents isn't cool.

Teenagers usually belong to a clique and seek entertainment in numbers. Some may belong to two groups, one for dating and another for general activities. Early adolescents prefer the somewhat formalized peer clubs, while those a bit older hang out together, have gatherings (parties) and group dates. Older adolescents tend to strike out with one or two friends or alone. Some adolescents confound the description by exhibiting behavior totally inconsistent with the above.

Caution Is in Order

A danger of affixing observed characteristics, based on a few, to an entire group is that the few may not truly represent the group. Your observations may be distorted by preconceived notions based on partial facts, myths, hearsay, and sampling error. Even scholars are sometimes guilty of prejudging a person based on his membership in a particular group. The expert's own biases may intrude into his rational thinking processes and distort the outcome. He may actually be searching for evidence to support a view he already entertains. By selecting those "facts" in keeping with a foregone conclusion and disregarding evidence in opposition, he can make a somewhat convincing and documented case to the uninformed.

One can always produce examples to support a position, but in most cases, selective samples are not evidential but only illustrative of a particular point. A sample of the whole group in question is a more reliable route, but caution must still be exercised. Before reliable data can derived, the process must be subject to such factors as the numbers of people sampled, the randomness of the selection process, the skill of the investigators, and the quality of the measuring instrument utilized. Even with care, the results may be suspect.

Responding honestly to an interrogator, voters, before voting, may distort the predictive value of a query by changing their minds at decision time. Exit polls, with the a vote fait accompli, are therefore more accurate.

Some topics under scrutiny lend themselves to providing misleading information. Ask teenage boys about intimate encounters with the other gender and they are likely to inflate the quantity and quality of their experiences. This may still be the case even if the responses are written and provided in private settings.

Asking about a person's views or experiences is dissimilar to measuring fixed facts. The average scores in a standardized test in mathematics for eleventh graders in a specific school district could be calculated with precision. In the absence of fraud, performance scores can be measured. Opinions, however, are not nearly as reliable and are subject to the wording of the question as well as its emotional impact.

"Do you believe in God?" is a common query by both laypersons and pollsters. Most Americans, without hesitation, reply with an affirmative answer. Others, based on actual answers, find the question too nebulous and hedge.

"What God? The God of Christianity or Spinoza's God or what?"

"I don't know what you mean. I see the term 'God' as an abstraction."

"Sure. What have I got to lose?"

What is a parent to make of generally accepted views and statistics about adolescents? The answer, from this viewpoint, is little. As a citizen, you should be concerned with anything that affects society. As a parent, your primary obligation is to your own teenager. You need not develop expertise on adolescent behavior. A cursory review of current research is sufficient. You need to have enough of an impression to help your underachieving child. In so doing, you will have made a major contribution to your offspring, yourself, the balance of your family, and the school system.

Summary

Certain identifiable characteristics may be attributed to most adolescents, and some of these, at times, may be irritating and worrisome to parents. The postchildhood period is characterized by swings in his mood—sullen and self-absorbed one moment, friendly and interested a short time later. The teenager may be imprudent and engage in an action without due consideration of the possible outcomes and consequences, which may cause some difficulty at home or in school. At other times, he explores every possible course of action in minute detail and drives adults to distraction by continuing to debate a decision already made. This inclination, when he's so disposed, of carrying analyses to an extreme may also be a source of conflict at home. The argumentative teenager may make a monumental issue out of minutiae such as a routine household chore or a harmless remark.

Ever wavering in mood, the adolescent in family relationships and home responsibilities becomes quite consistent, however, in items of his own interest. He likes cars, at least certain kinds, particular styles of dress and hair, and telephones. At some period he is likely to join his peers in wanting to restructure society, not too difficult a task as he sees it. He may pontificate about ejecting the materialistic establishment, especially the old people over thirty (he doesn't really mean or believe this but it fits his simplistic scheme), and replacing it with a new order of equity and justice. He may follow this preachment with, "Dad, can I have the car keys and twenty bucks?" He sees no incongruity in his positions.

New Thinking about Adolescents

Investigators have found that the adolescent does most of the things already described but that, as in almost all other areas, each individual differs. The noisome behaviors described do not make the typical teenager incorrigible, a delinquent, or a threat to society. At times, it just seems that way to parents.

The maladjusted adolescent was more than likely also burdened with problems as a child. But now, physically larger and more independent, he can express his negative behavior in more serious ways. Parents considering corporal punishment must reconsider their strategy as they contemplate the size and musculature of their teenager.

The adolescent in trouble with the law probably has a history of petty mischief, and the truant usually exhibited these tendencies in the past. The period of adolescence doesn't usually bring new and overwhelming problems but allows festering ones to grow. However, some aberrant conduct of adolescents may truly originate in the present since atypical behavior can emerge in any period of life.

The newer approach to adolescence sees the period as one of dramatic physiological, cognitive, and affective change. The somatic changes within the youngster may cause concern if they're too early or too far from the average but should not be a major cause of stress, rebellion, and criminality. The hormone flow is equally guiltless where behavioral disorders occur. There is a much more rational explanation. The majority of teenagers may at times face problems that, momentarily, seem monstrous to them but are, in fact, temporary and manageable.

New understandings, by some, include a reevaluation of the role of the affect in learning. One protesting parent helped, inadvertently, to clarify this point: "Of course emotion in adolescence is important, more than ever before. It's always been that way. How can you say that the role of emotion is a new understanding?"

The role of emotion has long been recognized in adolescence, but the realization of the extent of the emotional component in learning is new. Adolescents may be quick to react emotionally to an unpleasant situation—perhaps too much so. This, however, applies to *behavior and adjustment*. The significance of the *emotional role in learning*, according to recent studies, cannot be over-emphasized, although it is still underplayed by educators. This is an error that parents may help to mitigate.

A third new angle of understanding is a concept introduced mainly by Piaget explaining how the adolescent thinks. Considerable controversy exists about the theoretical explanation of the maturing mind and some may reject the Swiss master's developmental stages, but arguably he opened the door to comprehending the formation of thought processes in the growing child.

Piaget espoused four developmental periods or stages of the human mind. The first period, between birth and two, he labeled *sensorimotor*. The child's behavior at this time is primarily motor, although some early conceptual thought may be detected. The next period, between two and seven, he called *preoperational*. In this stage, the child is utilizing conceptual thinking and developing language rapidly. In the third period, seven to eleven, the child applies a version of logic to concrete problems and situations. Thus, the period is called *concrete operations*. *Formal operations*, eleven or twelve through fifteen, finds the child reaching out and applying logic to a multitude of situations. The periods, Piaget notes, are not independent stages but are interrelated and overlapping. Individuals develop at their own unique rate, but the sequence of development is invariant.

The revised view of adolescent behavior that is a necessary understanding for parents—the involvement of emotion in learning—and the new thinking processes of the teenager are discussed in upcoming chapters. This chapter has described the characteristics of adolescents from the standpoint of adults, or *looking in* at the teenager. The next chapter will examine the view from the position of the teenager, or *looking out*.

Wrap-Up

The teenager resembles the rookie athlete on a team, that is, inexperienced but willing and full of promise.

The world the adolescent sees himself entering offers freedom and the pursuit of his desires, but his dread of the accompanying responsibility causes intestinal quivers.

The teenager's tormenting self-doubt can be shrouded by external bravado, and he can dilute his anxieties by sharing experiences with others.

The adolescent's unexpressed imperatives center around belonging and doing. He could be a leader or a follower in a group, but he must be a member. The group provides the security he requires in a strange new world of lessened parental restraints, unfamiliar events, and a new world perspective.

The teenager not only is being treated differently by others, but he feels different. His body is changing rapidly, and curiosities have become urges, some with an unfamiliar potency.

The teenager should be treated as a unique individual and not as a representative of a mathematical average. The general description of teenagers contains elements of accuracy, but superficial and minor characteristics are exaggerated. The vast majority of adolescents demonstrate acceptable self-control.

Teenagers change their behavioral patterns suddenly with relentless mood swings to extremes. Somatic, cognitive, and affective transformations are accelerating, making the adolescent period difficult to understand.

The adolescent can be very trying at times, but most teenagers, irrespective of behavior, never stop loving their parents.

Parents must learn to distinguish between annoying acts and dangerous behavior. Irritations are temporary and do not alter the lives of their children.

The mental operations of the adolescent start to change from the operations on concrete objects and events of middle childhood (ages seven through eleven), which has consequences for behavioral adjustment and overcoming learning deficits.

Everyone recognizes the high pitch of emotionality in teenagers in terms of their attitude and behavior, but the emotionality involved in terms of learning has been substantially overlooked. Thus, the major cause of scholastic underachievement is ignored.

5

Looking Out

The View from the Underachiever

The world looks somewhat different to the adolescent than to his mature parents and teachers. He sees and hears the same sights and the same words, but he lacks the experience of dealing with the situations he confronts. He interprets happenings from an emotional base that differs somewhat from that of adults.

In this chapter, we'll look at the world of the adolescent, and especially the underachiever, from *his* perspective. Fantasy sometimes distorts his thinking and extreme sensitivity sometimes causes reactions disproportionate to the event.

The teenager is searching for meaning in life, and he wants satisfactory answers to the questions that haunt and confuse him. He is recognizing, rather quickly, that such responses are not always forthcoming. He realizes the importance of his future but he is overwhelmed with the present. In his view, that is enough to deal with. To him, a few years is a long time. If one listens carefully, records his words, and organizes them into categories, a very real picture of the twelve- to fifteen-year-old emerges.

Fantasy over Reality

"Did you study for the test?" Bart asks matter-of-factly.

"Sort of," comes Red's laconic reply.

"Me, too." Bart continues strolling alongside his friend, heading for the park. "Do you think we should go home and maybe look over that stuff together?"

"No, what's the difference? We'll both pass. We always do."

"My dad's on my case," Bart starts to explain. "He keeps after me. Questions. Lectures. Questions. Lectures. Like it never stops. Do better, do better, do better. Sounds like a motor with noisy valves."

"Got the same thing," Red adds.

"Why are they like that?" queries Bart.

"Fathers?"

"My mother is like that too," Bart explains.

"Parents want the best for their kids. It's natural," opines Red.

"Do they know what's best?" Bart asks.

Red stops to think. Seeing a stone about one inch in circumference, he bends over, picks it up and pitches it to an imaginary catcher. "Fast ball. Down the middle. Strike one!"

Bart brings him back to the subject. "What do you think?"

"I don't think they know what's best for themselves. At least, my parents don't. My father is always complaining about his boss. 'Doesn't know which end is up,' he says."

"Maybe he's right," Bart suggests.

"Well, maybe. But that boss-guy built the business. He started with nothing. Maybe he doesn't do everything my dad thinks he should but look who is the owner and who is the worker."

"Oh, I don't know. My father sounds right when he talks, but I guess you have to do more than talk in this world," Red observes.

"Do you still want to be an astronomer?" Bart asks. A casual eavesdropper would have thought Bart was changing the subject. Red knew that he wasn't.

"No, I guess not. You know? I don't know what I want to be," Red replies sadly.

"How about a stud?" Bart suggests with enthusiasm.

Red's eyes reveal interest. "Maybe I should be a movie star with all that money and all those starlets looking for favors."

"Great idea," Bart joins in.

Both boys continue on their journey to the park, minds enmeshed in fantasy land. Their interest is ratcheted up several levels as they consider the exciting possibilities of successful careers in show business. The upcoming test in school is forgotten. One moment they see life with a penetrating understanding. A moment later, they block out the real world.

Reality Understood

Earlier, we described adolescent characteristics mostly in terms of how adults perceive their behavior and how these characteristics might affect schoolwork. In this chapter, the world is being examined from the kid's standpoint. The major caveat, usually understood and usually forgotten, is that although they have many characteristics in common, adolescents do not fit neatly into pre-sized boxes; they, too, are individuals. Therefore, it may be specious to express such dogma as "This is what adolescents do" or even "This is what adolescents do in a given situation." Although the behavior of adults is also sometimes difficult to predict, the fully matured person is not undergoing the accelerated modifications of adolescence. The mood of the teenager is characterized by changes. Whether professional or parent, prognostications regarding adolescents have to be hedged. It is more accurate to say, "This is what most adolescents may do" or "My kid, in these circumstances, will probably do this." If, following earlier guidelines, you have assessed your child with a reasonable degree of accuracy, your predictions will frequently be on target. You'll also be wrong occasionally. Expect no more.

At about twelve years of age, sometimes earlier, the youth leaves the world of childish make-believe and enters the world of adult make-believe. In other words, in middle childhood (concrete operations), the youngster, although he knows he's just playing a game, allows his fantasies to blossom freely.

Eight-year-old Jimmy can hardly contain his excitement when he dons the magic cape that allows him to "fly." This is the best of all his Christmas presents, although other gifts were more expensive. His father watches him whirl about the living room claiming that he can see for thousands of miles from an imaginary height. Jimmy rattles on and on as if holding a discourse with the world's population on his amazing flying capabilities. His father is trying, with great difficulty, to construct the "easily assembled, no tools necessary" bowling game he has bought for his youngster and pays little heed to the words of the child.

A change of location of Jimmy's voice interrupts the man's concentration on the directions accompanying the tenpin set. Sensing something amiss, he is startled to see his child at the top of the stairs announcing to all that he is now higher than any airplane can fly and that he is about to demonstrate how quickly he can land.

"Jimmy!" his father warns emphatically. "You know you really can't fly with that cape."

"I know," mutters the youth, irked by this needless intrusion into his fantasy world. With arms outstretched he descends the stairs emitting a hissing noise as he "slices through the air."

Children at this age are aware of the difference between make-believe and the real world. They don't jump from dangerous heights draped in magic capes. They pretend to do so.

Sensitivity over Reality

When adults cannot distinguish reality from fantasy, they are labeled psychotics. But in varied ways in everyday life, the normal person has learned to avoid upsetting a tranquil situation by not expressing his real thoughts or by suppressing his doubts about the veracity of an event, a concept, or a generally accepted fact. One illustration of an adult attribute is sensitivity toward others.

"Yes, I just love that bracelet. Is this the first time your husband has bought you jewelry?"

"Your grandchildren are just adorable. Do you have more pictures with you?"

"No. I don't think you're too heavy to wear that yellow dress, but I do like the other one so much. You look good in black."

Playing adult games extends beyond avoiding hurting people's feelings and encompasses almost everything in life. Adults have learned the art of finesse or at least some measure of it. They've mastered devices to avoid discomforting situations whenever possible.

"No, really, I'm sorry. I would love to see the tapes of your trip, but Harry is expecting an important business call. Let me call you when we have some free time."

Tact is an adult attribute, not employed with equal skill by all, but utilized, at times, by most.

The Search for Reality

The adolescent is rapidly developing the ability to be sensitive in a given moment but has insufficient experience in handling delicate situations. Tact is not his strength.

The thinking processes of the teenager are changing quickly, and he begins to consider the thoughts and feelings of others to a much greater extent than in the past. When his mother says not to mention Aunt Susie's missing front tooth, he grasps the reason for such thoughtfulness. A few years earlier, even being forewarned, he might have blurted, "Aunt Susie, you look funny without a tooth right there." Now he realizes that his prudence will avoid hurting someone's feelings. He is learning to play the adult game.

The adolescent begins to question explanations that no longer seem satisfactory to him. He challenges answers that fail to satisfy his curiosity. As a child, he might have accepted, "You're too young to understand that. When you get older you will." Now he feels, rightly so, that he can grasp complex issues. He notices, however, that canned answers do not erase his doubts. The weaker the responses are to his queries, the more widespread and deeper his skepticism becomes.

He has heard, since he can remember, about "growing up," but now reaching that exalted state of maturity, he finds it, in some meaningful way, disappointing. The freedom to act according to his wishes is interlocked with the burden of responsibility for the consequences of his actions. Earlier, he felt the certainty of intelligent decisions as his parents determined the boundaries of his behavior. Now he is uncertain about accepting the responsibility of choice but, simultaneously, wants to try out his wings. One day, therefore, he will propel himself into a freedom flight, but the next day he prefers hovering near the secure and satisfying nest. If he wishes to avoid decision making and responsibilities completely, he might revert to a lower stage of development. At such times, he is, from an adult perspective, well behaved and compliant. Then, some seemingly innocuous incident, such as a phone call from a friend, may drastically reshape his demeanor, and, suddenly invigorated, he may surge through the house and out the door.

"Where are you going?"

"Out!"

"When will you be back?"

"Later!"

The adolescent is finding that parents, teachers, and other adults don't seem as credible as before. This reappraisal may be puzzling or even disturbing to him. His childhood world is now on a shaky foundation. Simultaneously, he discovers that his thoughts have as much merit as those of adults. He decides, with rising confidence, that many of his ideas are even superior to the people around him. Buttressed by this reevaluated estimation of his thinking prowess, he becomes cocky and self-assured, belittling younger siblings and criticizing parents.

Sometimes the confidence becomes timorous; he starts to feel apprehension about forthcoming challenges and he seeks reinforcement. He may handle this state of affairs in various ways. One possibility is to evaluate the power of his position in a practice range.

Mom, for instance, his subconscious determines, is a good and available target for your opinions. Fire some shots at her and see where they hit. If she disagrees, his inner voice dictates, try raising the volume of your argument. Maybe you can outshout her. If her stubbornness will not yield to your logic, inject some degree of anger. Perhaps, with persistence, she can be worn down. However, if she acquiesces readily, she is either patronizing you or disinterested in the topic. You can't have a good practice session debating with yourself. Try again later or with someone else.

Another good exercise, he tells himself, is to hold a discussion with friends. If they all agree, you're right. That's always a satisfying feeling. If some don't agree, you can engage in a fun-filled heated argument, which never seems to resolve anything but can be stored as ammunition for another time.

Finally, lacking the opportunity or the emotional state for either of the approaches, you can resort to solitude. Go into your room, perhaps take your pet with you, close the door, and play some good music. Turn up the volume. The music bonds you with others who feel the way you do, whatever that is. You're not sure of the problem, the complaint, or the protest, but you know that things aren't right. By locking the door and filling the room with sound, you've closed out that repugnant, unpalatable world.

Many of the youngsters, especially early in this developmental stage, find satisfaction with the common interests they have with peers and cling to groups for security and satisfaction. Many have more than one group with an overlapping of group membership.

Fifteen-year-old Jack represents a nontypical case. He is an integral member of multiple groups or crowds, as he calls them. In school, he associates with class members, walks through the halls with them, shares a tale at lunch with them, and meets some for extracurricular activities. However, when at home, he joins another group for playing ball, attending movies, cruising the mall, and sometimes for a common effort on homework. He explains this latter activity with his neighborhood friends instead of his school chums as being obvious. "They're here." Geography is a factor.

Jack's third collection of friends is reserved for dating. His weekend crowd, with the exception of one friend who is also in his after-school group, are the buddies he makes plans with for Friday and Saturday evenings. Jack feels comfortable with his number of friends. When asked how he makes these arrangements, he replies "I don't know. Just seems to work out."

Jack even has a fourth group—albeit smaller—which characterizes him as nontypical. These boys meet only by formal arrangement and not very often. The meetings are for the purpose of discussing matters about religion, philosophy, and anything that touches on the nature of the universe.

"If you're interested in these subjects, Jack, why don't you discuss them with your other friends?" asks the interviewer.

"The other guys don't seem to be too interested. Any time something comes up along these lines, they talk for a minute or two and then drop it."

"Your 'discussion' group talks at length?"

"Yes. But there's only three of us and sometimes Bob comes. He's a fourth, but he can't always find the time."

"Do you have any of these discussions with your parents?"

"No."

"Why not?"

"They have all the answers."

"Maybe they have. What's wrong with that?"

"There are no answers."

A similar skeptical or challenging reaction may sometimes be found in another, somewhat larger segment of the teenage population who demand explanations and justifications relating to morals, politics, and institutions in general. Even adolescents not overly concerned about such matters may have their interests piqued rather easily if they detect a personal involvement.

"The governor says he'll veto the bill mandating that public schools distribute condoms, but the speaker of the state assembly says there are enough votes in both houses to override a veto."

The Future Is Now

Many adults are concerned about structuring adequate savings and retirement plans even if they don't have plans to retire for the next thirty or forty years. They are perplexed by adolescents who exhibit such little interest in events that will shape their lives only five or even two years away. To the youngster, a few years is a long stretch, which is not unreasonable if time is judged as a percentage of their lives. A child just turning fourteen and entering ninth grade has four very long years ahead before graduation. This time span is equal to almost thirty percent of his life. He may argue that he'll worry about college when he gets a lot closer to it. It's too soon now.

His parents' concern for his far-away future is distorted because of the time element he feels. Meanwhile, the change from childhood to early adulthood has arrived. He has things to do and places to visit and new interests to explore. Now.

Finding His Place

The adolescent may be uncertain of himself, but he has friends with similar feelings, which provides the courage of numbers. He is issued without effort, merely by virtue of his age, a complimentary pass into the teenage culture of his day. The membership confers on him the esteemed status of belonging and the exalted privilege of wearing the uniform of the era, in terms of clothing and hair style and color. These are all badges designed to express conformity with the group and independence from the mainstream. The attempted result is the appropriation of the motto of the United States, *e pluribus unum,* and its application to teenagers.

The adolescent finds himself tethered to three systems of support while he seeks to establish an understanding of the environment and an identity for himself. He still has his home base for sustenance and a fall-back position. He has school, his chief workplace, which may not always please him but provides a familiar setting. Also, imbedded on some mental structure is the notion that school is there to help him. He has his teenage friends and culture, which provide him with membership in a large community.

The teenager tries in various ways to find a niche for the long term. Most of his endeavors fall within acceptable bounds, but, if the ties are not too strong to his home or school, he may break loose before his decision-making capacity is fully developed. He can quit school, run away from home, join a cult, or worse. In such cases, he is no longer just an underachiever. He is in trouble.

The adolescent's mood swings are accompanied by shifts in desires. The adolescent, excited about something, wishes to pursue it immediately. He demands independence when he desires it. He doesn't, however, want to sever the cord to home base, because he holds some doubts about his ability to cope with every eventuality. He likes to know that a safe haven exists whenever he needs to reverse directions.

Adolescents Are Sensitive

With all the bravado, he is, largely, role-playing. He's trying to convince his peers, his parents, and himself that he's up to environmental challenges, and he's sensitive to any perceived suspicions that he's not. He develops an image of himself and how he'd like others to see him. Anyone doubting this image may be puncturing his anxiety balloon. He'll pop. He may argue with siblings, remonstrate with parents, and even engage in fistfights with peers. He may attack an acquaintance who uttered a slur or questioned some aspect of an ability that he wishes to project. The importance of some trivial incident is exemplified by how well he remembers it later on.

"It was just a neighborhood game of softball on a lot. We were all about fifteen and everyone knew everyone else. I was up at bat with runners on first and second and one out. Then I see Dean strolling in from his position in center field to crouch behind second base as an extra infielder. Lee, at shortstop, turned to Dean and asked 'What are you doing here? Get back into center.' Dean answered, nodding toward me in the batter's box, 'He can't hit one into the outfield. He hits ground balls. With me right here, we might get a double play.'

"Every guy on both sides hears him. Baseball wasn't everything to me and I knew I wasn't the best around, but some in that game were worse than I was. The insult was starting to wrench my stomach apart. I didn't say anything and no one else did either. No one argued with him. That made it worse. I never forgave Dean. I was a lot smarter than he was and I never needled him about schoolwork or anything else before or after the incident.

"Anyhow, with all my might and my best prayer, I swung at the first pitch and drove it deep into center field, where Dean should have been. By the time the left fielder retrieved the ball, I had crossed the plate with the only home run I ever hit."

"And you never forgot it. You seem to remember every detail. When was that?"

"Over twenty years ago. But there's more to the same story."

"Dean apologized?"

"No. Nothing like that. I overheard Gary, who was pitching, tell another friend that, hearing Dean's remark, he purposely threw the ball right down the middle of the plate slightly high to give me a chance. He knew I did better with pitches up a bit. Dean took the blame for being out of position. We never discussed the incident, but Gary's a guy I'll like and respect forever."

Certain incidents, inconsequential to adults, may become part of an adolescent's permanent memory bank because of his extreme sensitivity.

Anxiety

The contingencies of life present opportunities for anxiety in most people, although reactions vary in intensity on an individual basis. Some problems, such as waiting for the results of a biopsy, cause anxiety to most everyone, as do other life-threatening situations. Lesser concerns may also cause some anxiety, such as a college student waiting for the results of an important test or a job applicant waiting for notification that a position is being offered. Everyday living is replete with anxiety-causing situations, although most are of minimal importance.

The situation facing the adolescent is illustrated by the adult advancing in age, who notes, "I just can't handle that kind of problem as well as I used to." Perhaps he can't, but he has handled similar problems in the past. The adolescent hasn't. Adults may not face repetition of precise situations, but they do become familiar with classes of problems. These often bring forth remarks such as, "What I do in a case like that is . . ." To the adolescent, the event may not only be his first but, in his thinking, the only time in the history of humanity that anyone ever confronted the enigma he faces.

Parents sometimes misinterpret the nature of an event when the teenager appears distressed. Sandy was obviously upset when she returned home from her first date. She wouldn't respond clearly to "Did you have a good time?" and immediately headed for her room.

"I guess it didn't go well," her mother sighed. Her father, imagining the worst-case parental scenerio, felt the rise of anger.

"Who the hell is this jerk she went out with? Do you know his family?" Without waiting for his wife's reply, he leaped to his feet as if he were going somewhere but forgot the direction. "She's only thirteen!" he exclaimed.

"She'll be fourteen in two weeks, Joe. Just calm down. Sandy will be down for Sunday breakfast and she'll tell us all about it."

Sandy did appear at breakfast time in a somewhat jolly mood. Her father, who had a sleepless night, couldn't wait for the discussion to begin but restrained himself. The conversation at the table seemed to cover everything but the topic of interest. Then Sandy, as if mentioning an incident of only moderate importance, asked, "Do you know what happened last night?" The question was directed at her mother. Her father swallowed the food in his mouth, stopped eating, and full of anticipation froze in his chair.

Sandy's mother, by gesture, indicated that the youngster should go ahead and answer her own question.

"We were in this restaurant, Nick's you know, and I ordered chicken and . . . , well, the other things don't matter. Bob ordered a hamburger. Anyhow, I was really hungry and they bring this platter that wasn't bad but there wasn't much of it. Well, I scraped the meat off the bones as well as I could but I couldn't get it all. I picked up the bone with by fingers and ate it that way. So after a couple of minutes, Bob says, 'Kind of messy, isn't it. Wipe the side of your mouth.' He didn't smile. He looked disgusted. It was so embarrassing, I could have died." Adolescents and adults use different scales to weigh matters of importance.

Anxiety in the teen years may be caused by a multiplicity of reasons. These include (1) not measuring up to someone's opinion, (2) not matching one's own expectations, (3) being humiliated, (4) feeling guilt when violating a previously accepted value, (5) fearing failure, (6) fearing losing one's self-control, (7) fearing losing acceptance, and (8) fearing the future.

Teenagers want parental attention, understanding, and approval. Parental scoffing at their concerns brings resentment. But above all of the other considerations, they want to be taken seriously. They face more than "raging hormones" and bodily changes. Adolescents look out at the world encumbered by a host of anxieties and facing numerous unfamiliar situations. Interestingly, or perhaps pathetically, society has offered them little in preparation for dealing with cognitive and affective development.

Adolescent Quotes

The following section will help to illuminate teenage thinking about school and other directly related matters. The wording of the respondents has been changed to expunge unsuitable language, and the order of responses was rearranged. The content of the quotes is, I believe, consistent with the views of the teenagers who participated in the discussions.

A few subjects closer to social issues or physiological development were deleted except for references to "fear," which has a direct application to attitudes that affect learning.

The material offered is merely a simple guide to present some insight into the thinking of the adolescent underachiever. School performance, in this instance, revolves around and includes teachers, curricula, schedules, and parents. To the young person, the parent is part of the educational process, even though, on direct questioning, not one teenager favored such inclusion. On reconsideration, after discussions, the role of the parent was recognized and added to the learning program.

The comments included in this section indicate that the responses of the adolescent are of a surface nature and heavily influenced by emotion. In this respect, these young people are thinking immaturely, are extremely self-centered, fun oriented, and concerned with instant gratification.

The respondents don't necessarily agree on priorities or positions. They know they want some things to change but aren't adamant since they are uncertain about the specifics of the change. They dislike parental assertion of authority: "You will do what I say because I say so." A parental error can trigger a rebellion, although this might not be immediately obvious. The teenager may harbor resentments that will foster negative actions at another time. When these occur, the parent is at a loss to explain the reason for the adolescent's behavior.

School Teachers

"I don't like the teachers who don't care. There's lots of them."

"Some teachers are too old."

"We should pick our own teachers."

"I hate teachers who pick on you for not doing so well."

"Bad teachers put a guilt on you."

"Teachers sometimes pester you."

"I've had teachers who don't teach. They just tell stories."

"We have some weird teachers."

"My science teacher is retarded."

"Some teachers are mean."

"Some teachers try to scare you. Like everything you eat is no good for you. If it's not a vegetable or skim milk, I guess you shouldn't eat it. Anyhow, I still eat pizza and tacos."

School Recommendations

"Make school interesting."

"They need a better lunch menu."

"We need more time to get to class."

"They try to teach things you don't care about."

"We learn about China! I live in America!"

"You go to school all day and then they give you work to do at home. Too much."

"No one should have gym first thing in the morning."

"Why don't they teach what we want to know?"

"They need smarter teachers. Some of them just talk. They don't know anything."

"Teachers make fun of you if you have an idea of your own."

"We should learn more about the universe."

"They should teach philosophy and what people believe. What the world is all about."

"I learned about astronomy from television. Why can't we have subjects that are interesting?"

"We should study things like dreams and parapsychology." (She knew what parapsychology was.)

Parents

"I think parents should set limits, but mine think only of the clock. I could be doing what they're afraid of at eight o'clock as well as eleven."

"When you're told to do something, is it wrong to ask why?"

"I think when you're fifteen, you should have a lot of freedom. You should make up your own mind on things."

"I think parents worry too much. I'm not stupid. I know right from wrong."

"You should grow up knowing what the limits are. My parents nag. But they're nice. They're trying to protect me."

"My father keeps talking about when he was a teenager. Yeah, sure. Why did they have all those drive-in movies?"

"My parents don't trust me. I like to stay out late when I'm having a good time. I do the same thing whether it's early or late."

"They don't give me a chance to prove myself."

"They don't believe the truth. Only lies."

"My mother hollers too much. I'm always surprised when she just talks."

"Yes, my dad is good at making rules. His reason is 'You're under my roof.' "

"I get punished too much. I want to go out and have fun while I'm young. If I do something wrong, okay, I should be punished. But I don't think low grades in school are a reason to punish me."

"If you don't get good grades, you should take the heat.

You're not going to get anyplace. You shouldn't be punished by your parents."

"If your parents don't like your marks, they should help you, not punish you."

"Punishment makes things worse."

"I know I need good grades but I just can't get myself started. I'm afraid of the future."

"It doesn't matter what color my hair is. My taste is my taste. My mother lightens her hair. I don't say anything. And it's none of the school's business."

"I don't see what my choice of clothes has to do with the school. 'Dressed properly' to them means the way they dress. I don't think that old generation has much to be proud of."

"I don't think music is good just because it was written a long time ago. I like the music I listen to. It's supposed to be loud."

"My mother thinks I can't think."

"My parents don't care about me. My father will say 'Here's some money.' What he is really saying is, 'Don't bother me.' "

"If they don't have time for us, why did they have us?"

"It's like the time I was telling my mother about my problem and she seemed to be listening, but then I noticed she kept looking at her watch."

" 'Love you. Love you.' They say it all the time. But when you need them, they're not around."

"When I was a kid I couldn't understand the idea of 'tomorrow.' I would ask my mother, and she said it was the next day. Then, on the next day, I wanted to know if it was now tomorrow. She never could explain it to me. Now, when I go to her to talk about something, she says, 'later.' The 'later' is like the 'tomorrow.' It's never here."

"When I ask my mother a question about schoolwork, she says 'Ask your father.' "

"When I go to my father about a homework problem, he says 'I'm not going to school; you are.' "

"I worry about losing my parents."

"Maybe I shouldn't be this way, but I'm afraid of death."

Wrap-Up

Jean Piaget noticed that in early childhood the little ones could not understand why others did not see what they saw. For instance, if they were looking at a picture lying flat on a table, they didn't realize that someone sitting directly across from them would see the same picture upside down.

As children grow, they come to realize that reality depends largely on a person's perspective. This concept may be confusing even, or maybe especially, for adults. "Why can't you see that my political views are the right ones?" Many words could be substituted for "political." Reality is sometimes shrouded in make-believe for children and adults. The child at play knows he's making believe and may be annoyed at being told so. The adult submerges reality whenever it may interfere with the pursuit of tranquil living. Sensitivity toward the feelings of others is one reason, while the discomfiture associated with asking scary questions we'd rather repress may be another. The range of possibilities is unlimited, from "Is my husband cheating?" to "Is death oblivion?"

The adolescent may at times fall back into a fantasy world to cover his own neglect or failure, but as he matures he searches for an understanding of the real world. He easily becomes disillusioned when the answers he seeks are not readily forthcoming. He comes to realize that part of growing up means that he must adjust to situations as they exist and that he, himself, must select whatever answers best satisfy his own personal needs. He may never actually reach a completely satisfactory state, as attested by the number of adults who are still searching for answers and meaning in their lives.

In his quest for adjustment and freedom, the teenager is overly sensitive, fears the burden of responsibility, and grasps for support wherever he can find it. His home, his school, and his friends provide the platform he needs for stability, but he resents the imperfections he finds. His support systems, the basis of his strength, are flawed, deficient, and wanting in many aspects. To be an adult, as he sees it, trite or not, means he must stand on his own two feet.

6

A New Understanding of the Adolescent Mind

An updated understanding of the adolescent requires a more accurate view of his behavior, what he feels and why, and how he thinks. Chapters 6, 7, and 8 deal with this information.

Revised View of Behavior

Most descriptions of adolescents refer to chronological ages, physiological changes, and the furor of active hormones. These are the obvious characteristics of teenagers. Belonging to a specific age group, adolescents are growing rapidly anatomically as well as developing the sexual identification of their gender. Unseen but powerful internally secreted compounds are modifying their organs and influencing their behavior.

These descriptions are so generalized that, improperly applied, they may be deceptive. The thirteen- and seventeen-year-old have little in common. Four years or so provide for only a minimal difference in mature adults, but a forty- or fifty-month differential during the teenage years places these youngsters in distinctly different age brackets. The terminology of this period is too loose, and the range is much too broad.

The rate of emerging sexual characteristics differs by individuals, as any teenager can verify. The onset of adult-type attributes (such as early menses or rapidly enlarging breasts) arrives long before many teenagers are emotionally prepared for acceptance. Sometimes the change is delayed; the little boy in front of the line in eighth grade may grow to six feet. Hormones are, of course, being secreted, but the urges they cause can be and usually are kept under satisfactory control. Exceptions abound, and these, especially the delinquents and felons, draw attention to themselves. The teenager in trouble is a thorn to society, but other youngsters of this age group, the vast majority, shouldn't be branded as obstreperous, unmanageable, or intractable. They're not.

At times, some of this majority act without considering their own ethical standards or the consequences of their acts, but their transgressions tend to be negligible. As one high school student noted, "I'm careful to avoid involvement in anything that could bring me trouble, yet some of my best friends are teenagers."

Thieves?

After school one Friday, Mickey and his friend Al decide on a circuitous but scenic route home through a less-than-successful business street. Looking around as they talk, Mickey notices a fluorescent sign hanging uselessly over a vacant store.

"Look at that."

"Boy, could we use those lights," mutters Al. "What a waste."

"We sure could," agrees Mickey. "They would fit into our model perfectly." Mickey grows silent as the two stare at each other.

"What are you thinking?" asks Al.

"You know what I'm thinking."

"No," says Al. "We better not."

"Why not?" Mickey follows up.

"They don't belong to us."

"Who owns them? The store's empty. Some kids will throw rocks at them. Break them. Look at the top one. It's cracked already. The rest will soon be the same way."

"Unless we liberate them?" offers Al, wanting to be convinced.

"Here, give me a hand," Mickey orders. "I can climb up a bit and grab the lower bulbs and hand them down to you."

"Okay," agrees Al. "But let's do it fast."

As Mickey elevates himself and reaches for a fluorescent light, a police car traveling to nowhere in particular turns into the street.

The family conference, as it is designated, is converted into a tribunal wherein Mickey's mother unleashes her fury at her hapless teenage son, the thief. The father tries to calm his wife, but she hasn't yet adjusted to the shock of the black and white parked in front of her house while the uniformed law officer stood in front of her door, Mickey at his side, explaining the offense.

"He was stealing. Actually stealing. I can't believe it. The humiliation. The scandal. Everything I tried to teach him is gone. Imagine. He was brought home by a policeman, I . . . ."

Mickey's father, becoming agitated, interrupts her. "I know. You already told me."

The man turns to his son. "Why did you do it? You can't just take someone else's property—not morally, that is."

"I know," whispers the remorseful teenager. "I just thought no one wanted those bulbs. Al and I did. At the time, it seemed all right."

"You're lucky that cop didn't run you in and book you, or whatever they do, instead of bringing you home. Then you would have a criminal record," Mickey's mother blurts out.

The incident in Mickey's home soon faded into a conversation piece, but the memory is indelibly imprinted on Mickey's memory structures. He feels more than contrition; he feels guilt.

Had Al and Mickey chosen to run when the police officer approached, they might have been apprehended, arrested, and charged with a misdemeanor. The decision of the boys to remove the bulbs was not part of a pattern. Their actions indicated only a momentary lapse of intrinsic restraints, not unheard of in adolescents trying to assemble their behavioral proclivities into a workable system. Many teenagers commit a few offenses at times but are hardly guilty of the horrendous acts sometimes associated with a generalized view of adolescents. An occasional infraction of acceptable comportment does not indict today's youth. As a parent, you should not expect serious misbehavior from your teenager as a matter of course. The shocking statistics reflecting teenage conduct refer to a relatively small percentage of the population, and most of these can be accounted for by the egregious environmental conditions in some inner cities.

As a parent, you should be aware that these exaggerated descriptions of a minority of adolescents tend to obscure the characteristics of the majority. The media has a tendency to report on an attention-grabbing but unrepresentative sample, thereby providing the viewer, listener, or reader with an unintended, yet slanted view of the true picture.

Using controversial headlines in print and teasers on TV, journalists often present their personal conclusions before presenting the facts. Anyone wanting to paint a picture of the contentious, bellicose, and irresponsible teenage population can easily find live illustrations and "experts" to support their view. Two essential elements of the picture are apt to be overlooked or minimized. The adolescents who fit the portrait on any continuous basis are an extremely small percentage. The balance of the adolescents usually demonstrate undesirable characteristics only during the infrequent extremes of mood swings, if ever. Describing adolescents in general as defiant and combative is not only disingenuous but perilous. The unwarranted disparagement of the entire community of teenagers, especially in school, leads to a warped interpretation of challenges facing the nation followed by implausible remedial suggestions.

A youngster, Ted, accompanied by two friends, Bill and Jim, enter a dry-cleaning establishment to retrieve some garments. A man behind the counter is counting out change for a customer who has handed him a twenty-dollar bill. The man presents the money to the customer, thanks her for the business, and turns to Ted, who presents him with a receipt. The man notes the number on the slip and responds, "I think it must be ready but it isn't bagged yet. I'll have to go to the back and get it for you. Just be a moment." He then begins to wade through racks of clothes on his way to the rear of the store.

"Look," says Bill. "He left the cash register open." The other two look. The man had given the drawer of the register a shove but apparently without sufficient force to close it. The drawer is ajar. Bill, who has noticed the careless act, points to a compartment which seems to be filled with ten-dollar bills.

"He put the twenty the lady gave him under the stack there. Must be a bundle."

"I could use a bundle," Jim utters in suppressed tones.

"How about half a bundle?" asks Ted laughing, as if it were all a joke.

"Maybe just some twenties. Whatever is under those tens," Bill suggests, and he looks first at Ted and then at Jim.

"He'll never miss anything until he counts the bucks at the end of the day," Jim says with a modicum of seriousness in his voice.

"Where is he?" Ted asks as he looks for the man at the back of the store.

"Out of sight," Bill answers. "He can't see us."

"Well," says Bill, "There's a long weekend coming up with Labor Day and all. Some fresh bread could satisfy my appetite."

The three exchange knowing looks.

The clerk returns to the front of the store carrying Ted's garment covered with plastic. "Okay, fellows. Sorry for the delay. We're a little busy, you know, with the holiday and all."

Ted hands the clerk the exact change, lifts his suit off a metal hook and the three boys start for the door. The man puts the money into the register, oblivious to the fact that it is already open. The boys leave.

BILL: I didn't think they kept that much money on hand.

TED: Kind of dumb.

JIM: Yeah. What kind of jerk leaves the cash register open and walks away from it?

TED: Dumb thing.

BILL: Maybe that guy just works there. Maybe it's a chain. You know, a big one. Maybe that guy just doesn't care.

TED: He's got to care. If it's his business, it's his money. If he's a worker, he's responsible for it. Just dumb.

BILL: Suppose some people came along and cleaned out the whole register? What would that guy have done?

JIM: He'd have to make up the money, that's what.

BILL: It would be a lot to make up.

JIM: Well, he's lucky.

TED: Sure. We could have cleaned him out. Or at least taken some money.

BILL: Why didn't we?

TED: Maybe we're dumb or maybe because it just wasn't right.

JIM: Yeah. Maybe. Suppose he's got a family. You know, kids and a dog and everything. He'd have to make up that money out of his salary.

TED: You know, he'd look bad to his boss, unless he owns the business. If he owns it, he might not be able to pay all his bills. In business, you've got to pay your bills. They cut off your credit. No credit. No business.

JIM: He seemed like a nice guy.

BILL: Look at this twenty my Dad gave me. It's got a lot of pin holes in it. Wonder why? Do you think we ought to go back and tell him he better shut that register?

JIM: No. He's on his own. I could have used some extra money. Anything would have helped. I think those pin holes make a pattern. Hold it up to the light. See. It does.

BILL: That guy ought to close his cash register drawer.

TED: Those holes do make a pattern. Let's see. The light comes through and makes a shape. You know, if you did things that hurt other people just because you could get away with them, it would be a lousy world—even lousier than it is.

JIM: Some guys would have grabbed some loot.

TED: Sure, but that wouldn't have excused us. You've got to do whatever is right.

BILL: The golden rule stuff, eh?

TED: Something like that.

Children under eleven or twelve follow rules because they may be punished if they don't or because they've been conditioned to do so. They do things because "It's right." Analysis is not necessary. It's wrong or it's right. Rarely is it dubious.

As youngsters approach adolescence they tend to interpret rules in light of society's needs. They see regulations as a necessity for order in the environment. They understand that without rules imposed by authorities, they would be living in chaos. The concept broadens. They see rules as a means to protect everyone's rights, not just their own. They see the effects of lawlessness and become reluctant to inflict harm on others. The values taught earlier are obeyed not only because it's part of their training but because they have gained an understanding of ethical principles. They project their thinking and their feelings beyond themselves to others. They weigh the consequences of their actions on others, even strangers. They utter statements of explanations such as "because it's right," comprehending what "right" means. They also grasp reality: a prudent person locks his cash register.

Teenagers, admittedly, are sometimes egocentric and quarrelsome, but they are also loving, caring, and interested youngsters eager to identify their own selves and status and eager to strive for a personal and satisfying goal. Despite their raging hormones, they usually function within the acceptable boundaries decreed by their parents. If the current generation engages in frowned-upon and frightening activities (i.e., sex, drugs), it's because society as a whole is engaging in these same activities.

The expanding new thinking about teenagers, therefore, encompasses the view that the vast majority of junior adults are well adjusted, morally fit, and law abiding. Both the on-and-off rebelliousness and seeming hostility are part of the learning and adjustment process, not a sign of moral decline. The adolescent understands acceptable demeanor, and, furthermore, he agrees with it, despite occasional slips. He's testing the waters, not drowning in them, which is a natural consequence of his maturing process.

Two misconceptions should be buried or, better yet, cremated so that they can't be exhumed. First, the adolescent years are neither carefree nor strife laden. Second, and to the dismay of the professional alarmist, today's kids are of the same caliber, although less innocent, as the not-so-perfect earlier generations. Where did Jack Armstrong and Andy Hardy go? The same place the replicas of Dave and Rick Nelson went. Nowhere. They're right here.

Wrap-Up

Many educators and psychologists have expressed bewilderment at both the professional and lay views on adolescents. Some young people can be found who will fit the "teenage" stereotype, but when this age group is examined as a whole, current research shows that the accepted descriptions lose much of their veracity. The reality is that:

1. The classification of all young people between twelve and nineteen as one group is grossly misleading. Each year during this stage of life brings substantial changes not only in the physical sense but psychologically. The activities of

young people past age sixteen and into their early twenties are not included in this work, which encompasses ages twelve through fifteen with an overlap at both ends.

2. The classic characteristics of adolescents are not inaccurate but should not be interpreted in the extreme for most kids. Alarming behavior on the part of a minority of teenagers, usually beset with severe environmental deprivation, tends to skew the statistics on adolescent actions.
3. Teenagers such as Mickey and Al may make an occasional error in judgment, and parent punishment is justified. Parental understanding is also necessary. Adults slip, too. The story of Ted, Bill, and Jim is not at all unusual. Teenagers, as a whole, are honest and law abiding. If earlier and current parental guidance is adequate, the adolescent will tend to resist temptation.
4. Negative assumptions and expectations on the part of society can influence the conduct of students in and out of school. Underachievement, for instance, is sometimes the result of a poor self-image resulting from overstated presumptions on the part of adults.

7

The Emotional Side of Learning

Despite its shortcomings and criticisms, the generally accepted measure of a student's innate ability is the I.Q. test. The intelligence test seems to provide the best estimate of a learner's academic potential. But how these possibilities are utilized depends, largely, on the degree of the youngster's motivation. J.P. Chaplin, in his *Dictionary of Psychology* (Dell Publishing Co.), defines motivation as "an intervening variable which is used to account for factors within the organism which arouse, maintain, and channel behavior toward a goal." Thus, the degree of motivation is instrumental in determining the utilization of native capability.

A student who does anything at all has some level of motivation in operation, but when educators speak of motivation, they mean in sufficient force to thrust the learner out of low gear and into high. The role of motivation is not new to learning, as any teacher can verify. From her courses in introduction to education to her graduate studies, motivation is emphasized as crucial to learning. Curriculum developers try to build motivational factors into the program to keep students interested.

Motivation, however, does not exist independently of other factors. It is an ongoing result of interrelated and operating emotional elements. Logic, derived from active cognitive structures—

the thinking mechanism—has some but only limited influence on motivational strength.

Motivation is the key to helping your underachieving child open his throttle, but, again, motivation is dependent on many elements classified as emotional. Each one of these elements has a profound influence on learning. Motivation, therefore, is intertwined with understanding, remembering, and solving. Emotion and learning are married and cannot divorce.

Jean Piaget opened many doors to understanding mental growth, but one of his most salient observations has been underutilized in schools. The Swiss biopsychologist stressed the importance of the connection between emotional aspects of learning and the thinking process. To succeed in a formal class setting, the emotional components of learning must be on a par with the student's thought processes. He argued that, "The emotional side of performance, therefore, always affects the thinking side."

The elements of emotion usually overlap, making it difficult sometimes to draw sharp lines between them. Emotions include feelings described as love, hate, anger, fear, joy, disgust, anxiety, despair, sadness, grief, happiness, and embarrassment. When any of these are in blossom, their effect on learning is easily understood. A mildly irritated student may still be able to listen, read, and study. But if he is overcome with rage, he is not likely to grasp a teacher's explanation that a hypotenuse is the side of a right triangle opposite the right angle. The teacher can forget trying to explain relevant calculations at this time for this student. Mild irritation and rage are extremes of anger, and their effects are quite palpable, but even the student experiencing feelings somewhere in between is probably also unable to function at his best in a cognitive sense. Anything beyond mild annoyance will likely impede learning.

This principle applies to other emotional states as well. A low level of apprehension may sharpen the wits of some students who may feel a bit jumpy in a test situation, but high anxiety is likely to hinder their ability to concentrate.

Interference in the learning situation may come from emotions not usually considered negative, such as "love." A teenager may overreact to a newly established pleasant relationship with someone of the opposite gender and allow his thoughts to overwhelm his studies. "Hypotenuse? What's a hypotenuse? I'm going to see *her* tonight."

A desired emotion, such as the feeling of satisfaction stemming from good test results, a promise fulfilled, or an invitation received, may foster good study procedures. These uplifting feelings, the result of being rewarded, recognized, or included, impact favorably on attitudes toward assignments. The homework isn't so forbidding after all. "What's so difficult about calculating a hypotenuse?"

Bad news may cause temporary debilitation, as expected, but some people react in the opposite way. Work, pursued with more fervor than ever, becomes the means to overcome emotional pain. Intense concentration on a task blocks out all other considerations. You can think of only one thing at a time. The passage of time is necessary for grief or some equally disturbing feeling to be diffused as it is assimilated into the mental structures of the individual. Time, presumably the great healer, doesn't always warrant its lofty reputation, but the afflicted person is given an opportunity to make an adjustment.

On the whole, disturbances do not influence learning positively. For most people, most of the time, undesirable emotions serve as an impediment to learning. Problems tend to intrude into a person's thought processes, retarding or even blocking any progress. Adolescents are particularly susceptible to predicaments and haven't as yet learned to cope with many of them. Serious situations such as the illness of a loved one will dampen the spirits of almost everyone, but a well-adjusted adult, unhappy over a canceled date, will still be able to get on with her life. The adolescent may view such an event as a life-altering catastrophe. "School? Who cares about school? My life is the pits." In trying to help the underachiever, the parent should recognize that emotion is completely intertwined with learning.

The underachiever automatically asks certain basic questions about his schoolwork that seem simple enough but are actually very crucial. He may be seeking answers, or the questions may be rhetorical. More frequently, the interrogatives are asked of himself silently for the purpose of clarification. The questions may be cognitive, involving a search for information, or they may be affective, asking how he feels about the topic. A parent may ask her child if he was thinking about one of the following questions, only to be told that he wasn't. Yet, he really might have been. In the mind, these questions are asked and answered at the speed of light. Looking at an assignment, the student is likely to ponder:

What does this mean to me?
Is it interesting?
How much time is involved?
How does it compare with other subjects?
Does it promise to be fun?
Will it be boring?
Will it frustrate me?
Can I really do it?
How are the other kids handling this?
What happens if I fail?
How will my parents react?

The confident student asks the same questions as the underachiever but answers and dismisses them in a second: "I can do this. No problem. Here's a way to go about it. Look, I've already started."

The comments of the confident student are conducive to successful task completion. The doubts raised by the underachiever become learning obstacles. The climate for learning is enhanced when the student's positive feelings encourage him to move forward and hindered when the student entertains fears of failure. The parental task is to build confidence.

Time Table on Emotions: Eleven through Fifteen

Just as anatomical growth rates vary, cognitive and affective rates vary too. The following, like a spring scale, is not intended for precision but provides some loose measurements for comparison.

Age Eleven

The darling has become an alien monster, seemingly able to move in all directions simultaneously. The child is careless, restless, forgetful, and sometimes downright rude. Fantasizing about the future is common. He likes to discuss himself. Arguing is fun, especially if a parent can be shown to be in error. He seems to be hearing a distant call for freedom.

Age Twelve

The monster has been defanged. The youngster is more even-tempered and less hostile. He tends to accept more from parents without a fuss. He's more tolerant of peers. He's now a seventh grader and unlikely to cause problems that stem from his behavior. This is a critical stage for learning mathematics. He may go to extremes in liking or disliking the subject. The opposite sex is becoming interesting; the girls, for the most part, are more advanced in their interest.

Girls start their giggling stage, which, for some, lasts into their twenties. In most other ways, the girls reach maturity in their late teens. Based on observed behavior, some of the boys, not a small minority, do not mature until thirty. Many women disparagingly claim, "Later than that."

At twelve, the child is beginning the process of abstract thinking and requires less investigation of the concrete. He likes to express his views but is not nearly as argumentative as earlier. Parents may detect a few warning signs signifying a growing dissatisfaction with school. He talks less about school, delays doing assignments, and hurries through his work. Not wanting to do homework on weekends is not a dangerous sign. That's common. Other activities are becoming intriguing. He's entered the stage of formal operations. Maybe. Some youngsters enter it later and some never.

Age Thirteen

The teenager is now at the top of the middle school, in the middle of junior high, or on the lowest rung in high school. In the middle school, he feels big and important. In the high school, he feels unsure of himself. Neither of these positions is an argument in favor of the junior high.

At this age, his nerves seem to have lost their protective covering. He is both negative and sensitive, an unholy combination. He responds to verbal barbs or even implied criticism with anger. He spends time in his room away from the family. He spends many hours considering his own life and his place in society, and he's uncertain about his role in the world. One of his few certainties is that others do not understand him. He is right. He doesn't understand himself either.

He's trying to assemble the loose pieces that constitute his life. He's trying to create some sort of self-identity. He sees, however, because of his entry into formal operations, that everything isn't just black or white, but that there are gray areas in life and that multiple interpretations of events and situations are possible. Certain subjects in school he feels are interesting, that is, those that focus on the cosmos, politics, sociology, and history. He belongs somewhere in this huge universe, but he's not sure exactly where. He is very defensive.

Age Fourteen

The ninth grader, in school, is trying to clarify the restraints imposed on him by his parents and school. He wants teachers to keep his classmates and himself in check and to make the subject interesting. He wants to push a bit and, if unhampered, wants to push more. He'll be satisfied, however, if he can't get away with anything.

One of his favorite pastimes is judging his teachers and their subjects. His newfound ability to think like an adult is being put to ever-increasing use. He's asking questions of teachers, other adults, peers, and himself. He's evaluating everything and he's highly critical. School is where it's at (friends, activities, and sometimes even his studies), but his parents are from a bygone age. He is energetic and wants to be involved in activities in school, in the community, and at home. Sometimes he realizes he has gone too far in this involvement, but he is now capable of laughing at himself.

He wants to belong and his peer culture is the big social club. He is learning the art of mastering life, including making decisions on his own. It's as if the game of life has commenced and he's a player now, full of exuberance. He's still learning how things work but he pretends to be sure. He's independent and engages in many activities with enthusiasm, but he glances back to be sure his home has an open door.

Age Fifteen

The fifteen-year-old likes the concept of independence with the security derived from a supporting parent—the same parent whose rules he flaunts. He enjoys debates and arguments and is exhilarated by proving a parent wrong. Proving them partially wrong will also do. He is still sorting out life and his place in the solar system, but parents can detect the influence of their training. He seems to have changed the clothes on values he was taught, but underneath the garb they're the same. The earlier parental teaching is alive and well. He's getting a good grip on his behavior based on an ability to analyze his own thoughts. He continues to struggle with his observations and analysis of society, but, though still highly critical, he's more willing to listen. He's almost ready for important adult responsibilities such as driving a car. He'll make this wish known.

Wrap-Up

The educational system is not structured to account for the emotional component of learning. Emotionally disturbed children are recognized, but emotion underlies the normal behavior of all children. Schools have tests for cognitive ability but no way to evaluate the state of a child's emotions other than on a subjective basis.

Emotions, nevertheless, pay a crucial role in learning and do influence the mastering of cognitive skills such as judgment, analysis, and memory.

Motivation, the prime mover in the learning equation, is intricately bound with the affect. The underachieving child, in most cases, lacks motivation, and, by high school age, if he's disinterested he's apt to stay that way unless an effective outside force is introduced.

Parents are in a position to supply the necessary ingredients of that outside force, which is something that the schools can't do at the present time. To do this, parents must accept some responsibility and, to an extent, get involved. Demanding, lecturing, and punishing an underachiever can infrequently produce successful results, although these are usually temporary. Mostly, these typical remedial attempts are doomed to failure since they do not take the affect into account.

Emotions alone do not account for learning. The cognitive, or thinking, components of the mind must be operating at an appropriate level. The next chapter deals with the intellectual aspects of learning.

8

The Maturation of Thinking

A Fledgling Adult

"Read those words to me again. The end of the sentence," ten-year-old Jeff requests. The frown, frozen on his face, indicates puzzlement.

"Let's see, Jeff. You said the last part of the sentence. All right. Here it is: '. . . as the ship plowed the sea.' Is that the part?"

"Yeah. Stupid. That's what I mean. Dumb."

"Why?" his mother asks, not seeing anything wrong with the passage and the sentence in question.

Jeff is happy to explain. "I know what a plow is. Farmers use it to loosen dirt so they can plant seeds. A plow makes grooves; it turns the dirt over."

"Yes, that's right. But . . ."

"You can't plow water," Jeff announced emphatically and triumphantly. He believes that he's right. Metaphors are still beyond his mental grasp.

At about twelve years of age, sometimes at eleven, the child moves from a stage termed concrete operations into a more complex period called formal operations. The thinking of the child now starts to extend beyond his simple ability to see, hear, touch, and smell. He starts to consider the possibilities that exist in a variety of situations. He begins to qualify objects by gradations of value or importance. Something is not just right or wrong but, possibly, a bit of each. He begins to see both sides of issues and recognizes degrees of good and bad. He begins to see things not obvious in a concrete sense, and not actually in existence, but which could be there under specified conditions.

The adolescent starts to consider hypothetical problems that may begin with, "What if . . ." He begins to think in the abstract —thoughts disassociated from a specific instance. He begins to view aspects of the world in conceptual terms. What, he may ask, is justice? What is equity? What does honesty mean? The blacks and the whites of his life lose their certainties as they turn gray. The youngster is beginning to employ a formal type of logic.

By the age of fifteen or sixteen, he has, more or less, completed the transition of his thinking from concentration on solid and formed items to engaging in abstract thought. The world has taken on a new hue, encompassing not only what exists, but what could be made to exist, that is, all of life's endless possibilities. The child, prior to the formal operations stage, utilizes logic, but only to a minimal degree. He views the subject, takes a guess, and plunges in with his efforts without examining all of the variables involved. In contrast, the teenager, faced with a problem, is capable of grasping all of its aspects, choosing the best available option, and anticipating the effect his choices will have on other people.

Parents take note. Your teenager, in terms of his reasoning capacity, is not the same child he was. His mode of thinking is changing. How you relate to him should change accordingly. Unfortunately, as with most human interrelationships, simple predetermined actions designed to fit all circumstances rarely work. That's why flexibility and adjustment are essential to living a satisfactory life.

Your teenager may not fit neatly into a pattern. As an individual, he'll develop at his own personal rate of change. You, therefore, must vary conditions to fit your child and not try to fit him into a preformed mold. The exercise of this aim should be relatively painless for a reasonable parent, except for the fact that the adolescent doesn't always want to play by reasonable rules. He is very apt, as noted under our earlier description of characteristics, to display wide mood swings, which diversify his behavioral pattern and make predictability exceedingly difficult. He also compounds this difficulty by demonstrating extreme swings in logic. One day he may reason as an adult, but on the next he returns to his finest level of immaturity. He is on a developmental elevator, perpetually going up and down. You never know for sure on which floor you will find him. Parenting isn't easy, as most parents will confirm.

In this new stage, the adolescent begins to apply his fresh style of thinking to himself and his environment. His newly overhauled psychological mechanism allows him to understand metaphors, unlike Jeff in the opening example. The adolescent starts to observe with a comprehension that stretches beyond the concrete object or event he is watching and allows him to draw inferences from incoming stimuli.

This new, mature thinking process allows the teenager to extrapolate from one item into possibilities not specifically mentioned. His listening transports him beyond specific words, spoken and written, to underlying reasonings not actually stated. He starts to generalize from one experience to other similar experiences. Thus, amorphous events of the past become coalesced into a framework that provides meaning to new encounters. His thinking carries him beyond the impressions of clever slogans to an understanding of the ideologies that produced them. The adolescent, mastering the top of the thinking hierarchy, expresses his skepticism and insights by statements such as:

"Yes, that's what he says, but what does he really mean?"

"Notice how he's changing the subject; he's not answering the question."

"He's got it wrong. That's not what those people believe."

"Sure, he predicted that one event, but he made other predictions that were wrong."

"Look. He's covering up. Don't let him off the hook."

Self-Scrutinizing

The teenager is adding his own thoughts to his audio and visual perceptions, thereby modifying their impact. He no longer so readily accepts information and views from authority figures. He now demands more substance, more evidence, and more logic. He can be convinced of things but not so effortlessly as in earlier years.

The adolescent is sometimes confounded by his own thoughts once he's reached the level of examining his own thinking. His own thoughts may be imperfect and require considerable refinement. He may, at times, isolate himself to mull things over and try to arrive at some workable, and acceptable, conclusion. When he's ready, he'll express these views orally to determine their strength. In so doing, he may irritate those around him, especially his parents. Tact is not yet his forte.

"Hey Dad. You know what you said yesterday about the mayor's tax plan? Well, you're dead wrong."

"Sorry Sis, but you don't know what you're talking about."

"Mom, you're all mixed up. We do things differently today."

Extending His World

The adolescent, in his new mind-set, is studying situations in the abstract. He is examining the nature, components, and impact of events. Unlike the child he was, who could reason only in terms of the present with a limited number of simultaneous ideas, the adolescent is exploring multiple possibilities without time constraints. A qualitative change is occurring in his thought processes. He doesn't require the concrete object before him and he's not locked into the immediate present. He can analyze where he is and where he might be going and has the facility to express his views with words.

The adolescent is beginning to extend his thinking to encompass the points of view of others and the implications of these positions. He doesn't necessarily accept others' beliefs, but he understands them. He now considers the ideas of other people, and he is becoming much more aware of their feelings. He is adding another measure of depth by taking their personalities into account.

Now that he can dissect his own thoughts, feelings, and personality, his view of himself is apt to change. He envisions himself as a part of society and comprehends the possible consequences of his opinions and decisions. He is becoming more conscious of his own abilities and more concerned about his place in the future. He wants to test the accuracy of his new introspection and the authenticity of his worldly insights by discussions. He is poking and jabbing at his environment and the people in it. He finds much of this intriguing. He finds much of it alarming.

Developmental Stages

Jean Piaget illuminated and described the cognitive transformation that changes a child into an adult. Many reputable researchers do not subscribe to Piaget's developmental stages (enumerated in Chapter 4) and opt for mental growth as proceeding on a continuum into more and more complex realms. The attributes of this period described by Dr. Piaget, however, are generally accepted. The disagreement is reserved for theoretical explanations. Detractors and supporters concur that the growth period is clearly not applicable to all youngsters. Some seem to take much longer in reaching the upper limits posed by the Swiss theorist. Some people never learn more than a modicum of abstract thinking all of their lives.

Despite the limitations of his theories and the focus on early childhood rather than formal operations, Piaget did open doors to new understandings that have influenced almost everyone in psychology, although not all would acknowledge this. Educators, once Piaget became popular, were quick to approve his notions but could do little, in a practical sense, to implement them.

The disagreement among psychological researchers has little relevance for parents of the underachiever, but the thinking structures of the teenager are basic to the overall remedial approach to follow.

The Result

The world of the adolescent is changing not only because his body is developing but because he sees it differently. When the child was seven through eleven (the concrete operational period) he was able to perform some early version of deductive reasoning but was likely to decide on a hypothesis without sufficient analysis. The first time some possibility sounded right, he was likely to seize it without further consideration. The youngster in formal operations is much more reticent about reaching conclusions. Perhaps, he thinks, some obvious-sounding explanation is not really correct. He wants to continue to explore and probe and not just accept the first reasonable-sounding answer.

The adolescent is starting to traverse a new frontier; he now has the ability to imagine all of the possibilities in a given situation. He can arrange propositions (organized statements), make reasonable connections between them, and through logical analysis determine the truth or at least the best answer. Where possible, he will try to verify his conclusions by experimentation. The adolescent's mind is starting to use deductive reasoning based on a hypothesis—a similar approach to that of a scientist. Mom, watch out. It, whatever the subject, is not right anymore merely because you say it is. From a parent's perspective, he's pursuing, exploring, and analyzing, seemingly without end. Crying "Enough already!"

may not shut down a debate. He's always ready for more. "How about if . . ."

Wrap-Up

As the child enters formal operations, his thinking processes are undergoing reformation.

The adolescent finds it difficult playing the classic adult game of "Do what I say, not what I do." He wants consistency in philosophy and behavior.

He uses statements for "shock value" to see what happens. He hasn't yet mastered discretion in expressing his thoughts. The reactions he observes will help him establish adequate controls.

He is starting to deal with abstract concepts and determine what they mean, their usefulness, and where they may be applied. Commitment, fairness, equity, justice, loyalty, and honesty are not just words but are growing for him in meaning. For example, to a young child, being religious means attending Sunday School. To an adolescent, it means how a person thinks and what he does.

The consequences of this cognitive stage include:

- Broadening interests.
- Exchanging views.
- Mental experimentation (arguing, debating, opening closed doors).
- Recognizing errors and contradictions in the positions of others.
- Questioning the decisions of authorities.
- Determining what others feel and think without relying solely on their words.
- Realizing that parents, teachers, and other authorities may not have all the answers and that some answers do not exist.

The adolescent is rapidly coming to an understanding of metaphors, is drawing inferences from what he sees and hears, is transferring his learnings from the original to new situations, is examining ideologies objectively, and is thinking about thinking.

This maturing youngster is going to school. Is the school ready for him? The next two chapters will examine the answer to this and related questions, with the emphasis on students who should perform substantially better scholastically. To help the underperforming student, parents should take a look at his school under a new light.

9

Schools for Teenagers

You have already assessed the academic strengths and possible weaknesses of your teenager and concluded that scholastically he does not perform at an appropriate level. You have determined that he is an underachiever. You are now ready to institute a program of motivation, learning skill development, and mental energizing. You will soon arm yourself with easily applied techniques to implement your plan and achieve your goal. It is clear that you are preparing to do your part, but what about the role of the school?

A remedial educational program, such as the one offered here, operating independently of the school your child attends, lacks an important component. Effective academic instruction requires a competent teacher proficient in her field and functioning in a favorable environment. The parent is not usually the person qualified to teach an involved discipline. Her role, in this program, is to help her child develop the affective and cognitive structures he already possesses and strengthen the techniques he must apply to promote a successful learning process. The subject matter he masters is part of the school curriculum. The two together, the process of learning (the parental effort) and the knowledge (the school's role), combine to produce an achieving student. Both elements, home and school, are essential. The more coordination between the two aspects of learning, the more successful the program is likely to be.

How good is your child's school? The answer is not readily forthcoming no matter what you ask or when you inspect. Many parents, before buying a house, inquire about the reputation of the local school. Most of the information provided, accurate or not, centers around the elementary school. The higher-level schools draw from a wider area that may encompass more than one economic level, which could be a factor in the quality of the school. For instance, the tax base for America's schools comes largely from real estate. The more taxes paid in the local district, the more funds the school board has for its system. Money is not the sole criterion for effectuating good education, but it is one important factor.

Schools in affluent communities tend to be of a higher quality than schools in average or below-average neighborhoods. Other considerations, concerning tradition, social status, political influence and such, are of import but not the subject of this work. The underachiever appears virtually in all schools, and that is our focus.

How are individual schools rated? The answer is varied, complex, and unsatisfactory, and we shall not dwell on measuring criteria. Instead, in this chapter practical suggestions are offered for the parent of an underachiever to assess the quality of her child's secondary school. She must know: If she fulfills her role, can the school do its part? Often, opinions about schools are based on some of the following criteria:

1. *Appearances*—The building, grounds, and their maintenance. The evaluator's aesthetic sense looms large.
2. *General impressions*—People develop a feeling about an organization without being able to note specifics. The personality and attitude of the staff plays a role.
3. *A good football team*—Ridiculous.
4. *College-bound percentages*—The higher the average I.Q. of the student body and the wealthier the parents, the higher the percentage will be. If the percentage is elevated

in a high socioeconomic area, that is normal. If the percentage is low in such an area, watch out.

5. *Percentage going on to status universities*—Same as above.
6. *Average performance on national achievement tests*—Are scores lower or higher compared to schools of similar student bodies?
7. *Academic credentials of teachers*—See section below on "Qualified Teachers."
8. *Views of evaluating teams*—The members are usually educators from other school districts and from universities. This is a reasonable approach, but weaknesses in the measuring instrument and in the selection of the participants are common.
9. *Blue ribbon committees*—These are usually composed of business and professional people (noneducational) and heads of community organizations. (See Item 3.)
10. *College admissions officers*—These are the people who know, but prudence sometimes censors their comments.
11. *Superintendents of schools*—Most of them can tell you. Most of them won't.

This list is not intended to be comprehensive but is included to help the parent ward off the confusion caused by the family maven who belittles your impression of the school with, "Oh, really? But did you consider . . . ?" You can tell the "expert" that you've considered enough. Two items, the second and the seventh, will now be analyzed in more depth. The general impressions you get of a school are subjective but, nevertheless, highly useful. Add to this the unstated objective view of teachers, that is, *their* thinking about the school. You can ask them directly, but a more reliable method is to check on the rate of teacher turnover.

The other item refers to teacher credentials, a misleading yardstick of competence. I can state such an opinion because I hold certificates to teach a variety of subjects at various grade levels, administrative certification, specialized graduate studies, and three university degrees. Credits are not useless, but the competency of teachers cannot be equated with the number of courses completed, awards, certificates, or letters appearing after a name.

A Parental Evaluation of Your Child's School—Teacher Stability

If the turnover of teachers is considerably higher than the norm in your area, you may have a warning signal that the school you are investigating is far from ideal. The opposite, where teacher transfer requests are rare and resignations even less frequent, is strong evidence of a healthy school doing the kind of job you and society desire.

The information you need may not be readily available, but if the school can't or won't provide it, contact the superintendent's office, the local school board, the parent–teacher association, the teachers' union, and the local newspaper and/or television station. You'll probably get more information than you can sort out in a week.

Teacher stability is one of the best ways to evaluate a school. No one, but no one, using evaluative measurements, tests, observations, administrative reports, or student progress information knows the school better than its teachers. Many, but not all, administrators are aware of this. I once knew a principal who described teachers as one step below angels. They're hardly that, but they know their situations. They can, if they're willing to talk openly, reveal:

1. The effectiveness of the school's curriculum and all extracurricular programs.
2. The caliber of the support personnel in the school, including counselors, remedial reading instructors, and other specialists, such as nurses, office staff, visiting supervisors, and anyone else involved in helping students.
3. The competence of the principal, assistant or vice principals, and departmental chair people.

4. The overall strengths and the glaring weaknesses of any and every aspect of the educational program.
5. The dedication and skill of every teacher in their department and many others in the school.

Individual teachers may distort some of the above points because of personal biases, but when their views are merged and averaged, they become the most reliable school evaluative criteria that exist. Teachers, unlike some other workers, are tied to their results and their efforts affect humans, not some widget or obscure customer somewhere. Teachers are in direct contact with the students and tend to gain immeasurable satisfaction watching "their" children learn. They also tend to become very frustrated when their efforts provide few of the results intended. Discouragement causes teachers to transfer to another school, retire early, or leave the profession entirely. The turnover rate of teachers, then, becomes a little-utilized but highly useful barometer of a school's effectiveness. Your decision about how to help your daughter or son should be influenced by the quality of the school your youngster attends, and that quality depends on staff stability.

Qualified Teachers

Teacher certification programs are based on degrees and test results. Few interested undergraduates fail to obtain teacher degrees, and very few succumb to teacher examinations. Advanced credits and graduate degrees usually translate into a higher salary range for teachers. The relationship between having advanced credits and degrees and teaching prowess is vague.

If I had to choose between a certified teacher and one without certification, without any other information being available, I would opt for the certified one. If I had to choose between a teacher with a master's degree and one without graduate training, absent other criteria, I would take the one with the credits. However, my selection would be based on percentage. A thousand teachers with special training, averaged out, would probably be better than a thousand without the extra work because of other considerations, such as interest in teaching or children and the desire for self-improvement. On a small number or on an individual basis, the effectiveness of teachers selected based on credits alone would depend on luck.

A master teacher is one who is an outstanding instructor, not necessarily one with a master's degree in education. Some impressive secondary school teachers I observed in the past had advanced degrees, but a similar percentage of highly competent instructors did not. In fact, some of the finest teachers I ever saw were in their first or second year of teaching without graduate credits and with only a limited amount of experience. As a parent, you would be wise not to equate the number of graduate courses a teacher has completed with the quality of a teacher's performance in class.

Instructors in secondary schools, as opposed to teachers in the elementary grades, must have a high level of knowledge in the field being taught. A master's degree in the subject speciality, such as mathematics, English, history, or physics, would impress me considerably more than a master's degree in education held by a high school instructor. The elementary school teacher, working with younger children, doesn't need an in-depth knowledge of the subject. She needs an understanding of and skills related to children. The secondary school teacher is faced with students who may ask penetrating questions and, detecting the superficiality of the teacher's expertise, may quickly lose confidence in her. The presentation of material, barely understood by the teacher, has a deleterious effect on classes.

Ill-prepared secondary teachers strain to make the content material interesting and challenging. The teacher, as a result, may become quite defensive. A student asking a legitimate involved question might be confronting hostility from a teacher who interprets the query as a means of revealing her inadequacy. Not sure of the answers, she may, as I have seen, employ evasive or disparaging tactics:

"We don't have time for that. Class, open your books to page . . ."

"We'll take that up at a later date."

"We've already covered that; you weren't listening."

"Your question doesn't make sense."

"That's a good question. I think you should check out the answer and bring a full response back to the class for presentation. Shall we say tomorrow?"

A teacher may escape an embarrassing query from time to time, but these teenagers are now in the formal operational stage of development. They are able to put themselves into the position of the other person and wonder why a satisfactory response was not forthcoming. Their logical conclusion? Cover up. She doesn't know the answers. They are, of course, correct.

Some underachievers have had unsatisfactory experiences with underprepared teachers. Some have been emotionally bruised by insulting remarks or frustrated by the lack of a satisfactory explanation. Their curiosity may have been dampened. One or two unfortunate experiences probably would have had only a minimal effect, but a continuous pattern will cause the student to lose all interest in the subject. Poor teaching motivates no one.

"When I don't know the answer to a technical question, I just say so," the high school instructor explained. Saying she doesn't know is a correct approach to handling these events, but too many "don't knows" will curtail the enthusiasm of the class.

Advanced training in technical areas is a valuable factor at the secondary level, but knowledge of the discipline is not the only criterion for evaluating the teacher. The teacher has to do her homework. The lesson must be prepared in advance for presentation to the class, at an appropriate level, and be stimulating enough to capture the imaginations of the students. Once interested, the class must become involved directly in the learning process. Provisions for the varying interests and rates of learning of each student is essential. Every class member should be comfortable with and understand the goals of each lesson and the entire course of study.

The whole practice of teaching is an elaborate synthesis of personal projections continuously modified by a network of feedback signals. People who want to teach must have some innate talent for instructional strategies and truly enjoy working with young people.

The answers do not lie in the number of credits accumulated by teachers but in their talent and their freedom to exercise their gifts in an accommodating milieu. As far as you, the parent, are concerned, the personality of the teacher is considerably more important than her university transcript.

Wrap-Up

Most of the time, the parent of an underachiever can work with the school in a common effort to improve his scholarship. The parent should feel comfortable that the school is capable of carrying out its expected role in academic instruction. She should not just assume that the school's instructional program is adequate. She should do some lay-type investigation of her own.

The usual evaluative criteria may not provide the answers required for the determination of the school's possible effectiveness in helping her teenager. She should not be deceived by formal or expert evaluations based on statistics. Rather, she should form an intelligent opinion of her child's teachers. Her own judgment, based on the suggestions presented herein, may be more valuable than all other criteria combined.

If the school, in her opinion, does not meet the standards she believes are necessary to help her child, she must, if at all possible, arrange for a transfer to another educational institution.

The single, most important consideration of the quality of the school is her youngster's teachers. If these teachers meet the specified requirements, they will also be cooperative people. The parent then, with her own efforts coordinated with the school's, will be in a successful position to raise the scholastic performance of her adolescent underachiever.

10

Why Schools Can't

Raison d'être

Schools exist for reasons unrelated to providing jobs for several million people. The function of the educational system is to produce a populace that can think logically, recognize and accept civic responsibility, and produce the goods and services necessary for a strong and ever-growing economy. An educated citizenry is necessary for the general progress of the country as a whole in all worthwhile fields, and, therefore, the schools must be supported by everyone.

If Mrs. Johnson's children have long since graduated and Mrs. Williams never had children, both are just as obligated to pay for the education of Mrs. Smith's children as Mrs. Smith is. The cost of education cannot fall only to the parents of the children receiving the services at the moment. For the well-being of the entire nation, the expense must be shared by all. Every child who fails to reach his academic potential reduces the level of skill available to the United States. Unbelievably, this skill deficit, according to test results and investigative reports, in effect, matches the national debt.

A quiet suspicion is circulating among some educators that the schools are somewhat better than test results indicate, but there is almost total acknowledgment that the system is falling short of today's educational needs. Every citizen, not just parents, should be concerned about everything that schools should do but fail to accomplish. This work, however, addresses itself exclusively to the underachiever in secondary school. School weaknesses may touch upon many different areas, but the focus herein is only on the adolescent who meets the definition of an underachiever as stated earlier.

The Classroom

The inherent organization of the classroom limits the free interaction of students, abridging their ability to exchange information and offer possible interpretations of data with each other. Students learn from their classmates at every age level, but only if such an opportunity is provided.

Children, in some instances, also communicate more effectively with a particular learner than does an adult. A lower-grade teacher, having difficulty understanding a pupil, may ask of another child, "What did he say?" and receive a coherent response. Some educators would consider this a no-no, but it can be done intelligently without embarrassing the child in question. A child will become more frustrated at being unable to get his point across than embarrassed or discomfited by having peer help. The other children in the room quickly accept third-party assistance from one of their own without undue concern.

The above scenario is only one example. Children in the right circumstances can help each other to learn, and it doesn't happen only with the young ones. College students often study together as do graduate students and young people in professional schools. Not everyone profits from such group efforts but many do. The nature of the classroom organization limits this type of activity. Most of the time, it's the teacher and the class in a learning situation, where the class is melded into a single unit instead of a body of individual learners.

Schools have tried various arrangements and approaches to alter this instructional handicap, but no such program has been generally accepted over the long term. New organizational concepts are created by thinking educators who momentarily excite school people, only to have the innovative procedures gradually modified until their original purposes are rendered meaningless.

Your child, as an underachiever, is probably not participating in an effective interactional program but, more likely, is in a traditional classroom arrangement, although it may bear a nontraditional designation.

Much smaller classes, as most teachers advocate, would provide opportunities for beneficial interaction, but the costs are obvious. Schools are having difficulty meeting present obligations. In the real world of educational endeavor, costs are a factor, sometimes *the* most important factor.

Educators recognize the importance of individualized instruction, but few can organize, monitor, and evaluate full-scale individualized programs. Such efforts are usually superficial, as the results indicate. Technology was hailed in the past as the knight on the gallant steed that would resolve the issue of student uniqueness, but it lacks a fundamental element necessary to be highly effective, as illustrated below.

Programmed learning, teaching machines, and computer-assisted instruction have been with us, in some form, for over thirty years. Programmed learning is similar to the software that feeds the teaching machine but stands on its own without an electromechanical device. The teaching machine is simply an early computer that uses a version of programmed learning referred to as software.

The reader may have trouble with the next statement, but take it on faith. Educators make mistakes. Really. For instance, a school district chose one school to utilize programmed learning when enough programs in various subjects became available. The school was designated as a model and opened to visitors. Interested people came from relatively distant districts to observe how advanced educational practices could enhance learning.

After receiving accolades from many quarters—professional, parental, and journalistic—the program was downplayed and quietly discontinued. No one ever pronounced the effort a failure, and when anyone asked a question about it, the person was referred elsewhere. What happened?

The interviewer, during the first months of the program, asked questions of one of the participating students.

"What do you think of using programmed learning?"

"Great. I love it."

"Are you learning the subject?"

"I'm learning all the subjects."

"What is it about these programs you like so much?"

"I can go at my own pace. I don't have to worry about kids who are holding the class back or those guys who are faster than I am. I pick up every day where I left off and I don't worry about the rest of the class."

"That sounds like a true individualized approach. Do your classmates like it too?"

"Yes. I think all or nearly all."

Had the interviewer been Sherlock Holmes he would have recognized the clue to the failure of the program, already presented.

Several months later, the interviewer questioned the same student.

"What do you think of using programmed learning?"

"It's okay."

"Are you learning the material?"

"Well, I'm not having any luck in some subjects. I think they're going to cancel the whole thing. I wish they would."

A visitor to the school when the approach was first initiated might visit a mathematics class. The class is in session. At each desk, a student, using a program, sits quietly, concentrating on the task in front of him. The teacher stands at the side of the room and, from time to time, moves among the students. On occasion, a student raises his hand and the teacher hurries to him. She then confers with the student in muffled tones so as not to disturb the others. The room is extremely quiet. No sound is louder than the turning of a page.

The visitor moves on to another class, this one in social studies. Each student is working at his own desk on his own program. The teacher stands in front of the class. A girl clears her throat—a sound somewhat louder than the turning of a page.

The visitor moves on to another class; the subject is English. Each student is focusing intently on his own page of the program. The teacher is sitting at her desk. The loudest noise is made by the visitor exiting in disgust.

The tendency of educators, as with television programmers, is to overdo a good thing. This particular school exemplified this inclination. Adolescents have trouble sitting still, remaining quiet, and maintaining interest in dry subjects for any time period. Programmed learning, as is television, cassettes, computerized instruction, or any technological delivery system, is useful to supplement the instructional program, not to replace it. The school in question watched in surprise as its students wearied of the individualized curriculum in almost every class every day. The performance of the students fell off, especially in terms of quantity. The students simply grew bored with sitting quietly, hour after hour, reading and entering responses into a program.

The programs are an asset if utilized strategically for a segment of the course. Individualized programs do not effectively supplant the teacher. Teacher-to-learner and learner-to-learner interactions breathe life into an otherwise dull curriculum. The model school expired as the end result of uninspired planning.

The limitations of instructional techniques available to schools are emphasized by the new insights, and some old ones, into the mind of the adolescent. Learners require student-to-student communication, and, as even prehistoric people discovered, they need a competent teacher. As modern people discovered, the teacher cannot be on television or a tape or a talking electronic device of any kind. The teacher must believe, actively working with the students, explaining, emphasizing, encouraging, and analyzing. The quality of the teacher, more than any single factor, determines the success of the instruction. For highly motivated learners, and for limited periods of time as supplementary material for specific subjects (e.g., foreign language), technology can be extremely valuable. For everyday education, across the board in content, and over time, students learn more from a live teacher.

Students are more comfortable with a human who responds to their concerns at the moment. Some questions can be postponed for a later time, such as why the colonists objected to certain taxes and not to others. But some questions require an immediate response, such as why the equation that should balance doesn't. In this latter example, if there is no answer the whole learning process may shut down until the misunderstanding is cleared away or a mistake is found.

Students learn from oral questions, answers to the teachers' questions, and comments from their classmates. New ideas arise by the amalgamation of individual contributions made by various members of the group. Students may help others indirectly by rephrasing a teacher's statements and clearing up nebulous points.

Because a student sits quietly and attentively at his desk does not mean that he comprehends a given concept. Many learners avoid speaking up for any number of reasons, such as:

- They may think others follow the teacher's explanation and do not wish to reveal their lack of understanding.
- They've just asked a question or two and are embarrassed to ask still another.
- By their nature, they tend to follow the class's progress and learn well but feel compelled to avoid active participation. Not all students, even good ones, are outgoing or natural leaders.
- They may simply be self-conscious at the moment for reasons unrelated to the classroom.
- Their minds may have drifted to a more interesting subject.

Teachers learn to read faces and differentiate between students who wear puzzled expressions, those whose eyes display a faraway look, or those who are paying attention to something other than the lesson at hand. The quality teacher repeats an explanation, attacks a difficult problem from another angle, and refocuses the attention of individual students by changing her voice and position in the room. Hi-tech gadgets can provide assistance to the educational delivery system, but the prime instructor is still the most competent teacher.

Class interaction can be a dynamic learning process in itself, and although it is not the only way to learn, it is a significant technique for teachers to utilize. However, as with other systems, this, too, should not be used all of the time in every class.

The teacher should be the one to plan a variety of approaches based on the subject, caliber, nature, and needs of the students; it is the teacher who should implement her own plans. The teacher, in a decision-making capacity, can modify the instructional program to produce the best possible results for the students at hand. The everyday controls of the learning process cannot be manipulated adequately from a university seat, the superintendent's office, the state capital, or Washington, D.C.

Schools cannot replace good teachers with standard or cable television, computers, updated textbooks, audio and video cassettes, or other hi-tech devices. Learning requires emotional involvement, but the importance of the degree of this involvement is only now coming to the fore. Learning equipment initially may stir curiosity, interest, and excitement in the student, but the stimulation has a limited life span. Much, although not all of it, gradually dissipates. The good teacher, the fulcrum of the classroom, in a good environment with students who have learned to work together, provides the best learning experience over time.

Interest can be maintained at a high pitch throughout a semester by a truly qualified teacher using a well-prepared course of study. This affect, although understood by educators, unfortunately remains largely ignored. Curricula may contain some phrases concerning motivation, but the emotional component of learning is intricately involved not just with the introduction of a topic but in mastering the material throughout. Yet, schools, under existing design conditions, can do little beyond that which already transpires in terms of motivation.

The school culture, passed on from decade to decade, provides passionless learning to its students without intending to. The new psychological knowledge about the place of affect in assimilating the content and process of education remains in a neglected category. The parent of a youth whose interest in school has waned can help the student regain or gain, depending on the history, an interest in learning.

Under heavy pressure to produce, schools follow paths that, seemingly, should bring results. They teach subject matter that can be measured by objective tests and then teach for those tests. Improvement in test scores indicates success and, therefore, that they are doing their job. The intellectual development of the student must take a rear position to the exigencies of the moment—high test scores. If the education of the student lacks comprehensiveness and usefulness, that is the price of outside pressure.

Underachievers who do not disrupt classrooms are not high-priority problems. Schools are evaluated on the basis of the average of test scores, such as the average number of graduates, the average grade on the S.A.T. scores, the average number of graduates admitted to college, and the average in national achievement tests. "The average score for our students is . . ." If John and Meg and Josh are well below their measured potential, that can't be helped. Someone has to be at the bottom, even though they may not belong there. "The individual is important," but, on the other hand, the district is measured by averages.

Wrap-Up

Teachers are paid based on a combination of the number of degrees and credits they've earned—though a proven relationship between college courses and competency is questionable—and by the number of years of experience they have. As one sage remarked, "A teacher with twenty years of experience may have only one year of experience—twenty times." Few school systems reward teachers on the basis of effectiveness.

Teachers are locked into restrictive educational programs with only a minimum of academic freedom. Innovative teacher efforts are curtailed by the need to be efficient, that is, to cover the material assigned. Teachers are hampered by nonteaching assignments and bureaucratic-type paperwork. Adolescents who do not fit precisely into programs prescribed by the experts may and do fall between the slats. The space between the slats is widening. More students are falling.

The innate high energy of the adolescent is underutilized in the current instructional design and is reserved for after-hour activities. Instead, many schools treat a teenager as a potential explosive force to be watched by bomb squads.

Schools have little provision for the affective nature of learning but substitute considerable lip service instead.

Some individual teachers have a grasp of the formal operations stage of mental development, but schools have not as yet redesigned their curricula to fit this psychological understanding. For instance, life is an ongoing problem-solving experience, but courses in how to resolve issues and critical thinking are lacking.

With a reasonable degree of accuracy, objective tests can measure the goals enumerated in a course of study. The criticism of the curricula in use revolves about their limitations. The programs fail to further the development of the overall thinking process, the development of the adolescent's ability to overcome obstacles, and the development of resiliency systems to help students rebound after setbacks. The problems of the underachiever cannot be seriously considered by the schools within their present, tradition-bound organization.

America's schools have much to offer a large number of students, but if your child is an underachiever, don't expect current educational practices to turn him around. Parents can provide the necessary remediation; schools can't.

Many of the subjects offered in the schools are not interrelated but amorphous lumps of information. Much of this is not transferrable, has little relevancy to the student, and, therefore, is boring. One underachiever describes his school as "Monotony Incorporated."

The school systems cannot be held accountable for not offering courses or procedures that are not available. Schools rarely create their own curricula. Teams of teachers and specialists usually cannot do more than produce sketchy outlines with some vaguely defined goals and objectives. As a general rule, they adopt and adapt programs from other districts, publishers, authors, universities, and specialized profit and nonprofit organizations. This is a workable method, except districts can't modify and utilize programs that don't exist, such as programs for the underachiever.

Those who attempt to depart from outdated teaching methods to provide for current needs in a changing world face opposition from vested interests and the uninformed. Innovation is praised as a word and decried as a concept. Politicians and, in a large measure, the public, too, hanker for the good old days of education (the scholastic Garden of Eden), but the student body has changed, society's requirements have changed, and everyone's expectations have changed.

School systems around the world will undergo momentous improvement in the twenty-first century. The United States, with its educational infrastructure in place and a university system more powerful than any combination of other industrial nations, will certainly play a part. Parents of underachievers, however, can't wait for a momentous overhaul. If you have a child in school, you must act now. The balance of this work will tell you how.

11

Assembling the New Understanding

The Conventional Parental Remedial Role

"I've talked and talked and explained and explained and have succeeded only in exhausting myself. He doesn't listen. He just doesn't listen."

The parent, knowing her child could do much better as a student, tried "everything." She couldn't get him to work at school or at home on his schoolwork. After realizing that just telling him was not bringing about changes, she decided on a plan to get him to study as he should. The first effort consisted of the sugar approach. She encouraged him to concentrate on his homework, offering compliments for everything he did satisfactorily, and then introduced a system of rewards.

"I thought I'd hit on it with the rewards. He started to pay more attention to school, and his grades showed a definite improvement. Then he slacked off and his grades declined. I increased the reward, but to no avail. I was just spoiling him without getting the results I wanted."

Rewards, intelligently utilized, may be a useful short-term, specifically applied incentive. But rewards in the form of materials or privileges are not likely to have a favorable ongoing effect. Intrinsic rewards derived from the satisfaction of a job well done, or material learned, or a skill developed are the only kind that provide long-term payoffs. Rewards in the form of recognition, too, provide incentive for continued effort. These rewards may be in the nature of good grades, prizes, jobs, salary increases, promotions, and, in certain situations, accolades and applause. The teenager's parent who provided extra allowance money and stay-out privileges found that this type of reward soon loses its effectiveness. There is always the exception, but most underachievers cannot be "bought" for an extended period.

"After the rewards fizzled as an incentive, I withdrew them and instituted strict disciplinary measures. 'You will do what I say,' I said. He didn't. 'You will do what I say or I will punish you,' I said. He didn't. I don't believe in empty threats, so I punished him. Grounded. After school. Weekends. 'You can work your way out of this mess,' I said, 'by getting on your schoolwork. As soon as I see some results, the punishment will be lifted.' I didn't lift the punishment because I didn't see the results."

Punishment sometimes has a positive effect on the underachiever, but, as with rewards, results tend to be temporary. An adolescent, eager to accompany peers on a special trip, to a dance, or to a rock concert, may make an extra effort to earn that right but, in most cases, will gradually return to his underperforming role. Pain killers have a salutary effect for the moment but don't affect the cause of the disturbance. Symptomatic relief is useful for the moment but does not replace a "causectomy."

"I gave up on the suggestions offered by various people and decided to go back to talking. I sat him down and tried looking at the whole problem. He was young, he had a long life to live, and he certainly wanted to live it in the best possible way. Even if he didn't like school, a good education was necessary for a good life. A good education affected his social life, his career, his standard of living, and his life-long satisfactions. There are other important things in life, too, such as health, but a good education didn't harm those other things.

"I asked him to comment on every point and he did. We discussed everything about school and why he should do his best. He participated actively in our talks, and whenever I said we should have another conference, he seemed willing.

"I used every form of logic I could and gave him every opportunity to refute what I said. He took issue with very little. On the contrary, he seemed to agree with every important point.

"The results? We seemed to be getting along fine, but his grades didn't improve."

Your teenager's lackluster school performance is not usually enhanced in the long term by promises, rewards, scoldings, and penalties. Talking could be highly effective but not where the adult is dominant. The learner must be involved; the specifics on how to do this will come later.

Reshaping Outlooks

Professionals in the field of human behavior agree in the main that reshaping long-held notions is a difficult and trying task. Learning is not merely the addition of new information but, very often, the modification of understandings already in place. The existing mental structures must change to accept the new knowledge. The parental role in bringing about these essential changes is discussed in the next chapter.

The effort to involve the parent in learning is not innovative, but the new thinking and unusual approaches, to a large measure, are quite different. The parent, in the first segment of this book, has been given two tasks. The first, and not radically dissimilar to some of the more updated proposals, is to think of her child as an individual and not as a typical representative of a nebulous age group in a period called adolescence. The other task is to become directly and considerably involved in her child's psychological development. Established views tend to cling tenaciously to their moorings, and phrases such as "psychological development" emit feelings of uncertainty to parents. Neither should evoke any level of trepidation, because all of the recommendations offered are doable by untrained adults and fall within the realm of parental responsibility.

The mere act of involvement by parents, absent profound errors, is likely to produce beneficial results. Humans, possibly because of some gregarious instinct, desire to be recognized as integral members of their household and community. When, according to their perceptions, this acknowledgment has been denied them, they may withdraw or become negative, spiteful, and antagonistic. Withdrawal could lead to depression. Belligerence could induce malefaction. People who feel ignored and forgotten are apt to engage in repugnant acts to redress their perceived deprivations. Your own child is probably not at either extreme, but if he feels, subconsciously, estranged from his parents at the moment, he will search for an acceptable identity, and he may easily become a scholastic underachiever. Parental intervention, therefore, intelligently discharged, could become an effective motivator.

Relationships are frequently strengthened by the mere act of expressing interest and sincerity. In the 1930s, the Western Electric Company found that efforts to improve working conditions increased productivity. In fact, whatever management did to help resulted in better employee performance.

The results were surprising until management realized that improved employee efforts were not brought on by changes in rules and physical conditions but by the sensitivity, concern, and recognition expressed by the employers. This phenomenon, known as the Hawthorne Effect, has relevancy in parental relations with their children. By offering active assistance and encouragement to their offspring's educational efforts, parents are already raising his achievement level.

Understandings

To be optimally successful, impediments to an effective program should be removed. Obstacles that frequently block progress should have been obliterated by careful attention to prior chapters. Parents, by now, should have discarded several ingrained views about young people and be ready to accept some revised thinking.

- There are a multiplicity of causes of underachievement, and some arise from the natural maturation of the intellect.
- Symptomatic remedial efforts, even when seemingly successful, are usually only temporary. They may actually be counterproductive by inducing frustration when the student realizes he is slipping again. Remediation must be directed at the cause of underperformance.
- The classic view of teenagers, where the averages are distorted by a minority, may result in misperceptions that, in turn, produce negative expectations in both the parent and the student.
- Parental expectations can be significant in encouraging underachievers to greater effort. As with everything else, the adolescent may question, challenge, and argue. If the parent holds his ground and produces data to show she is informed on the subject, the young one usually backs off of a confrontation and mulls over what he has heard.
- Parents should not rely on their own recollections of their teen years, which may suffer from major distortions and have little application to their child, a distinct individual living in another era.
- Remediation of scholastic difficulties depends on a fairly accurate picture of the learner as a singular being, not as a composite of many.
- The youth in question should be evaluated by utilizing all of the information available, not just grades, intelligence tests, or someone's opinion. Parental insights and observations should not be discounted.
- Adolescents exhibit certain characteristics that may be anticipated and understood. Updated information about teenagers has revised the general view of the majority of twelve- to fifteen-year-olds, enabling the parent to determine which behavioral acts fall within acceptable boundaries and which puncture the limits.

- Parental influence over adolescents has not waned but is not as obvious as in the past. The young person is questioning and challenging as a means of developing his own views and concepts. He still seeks parental attention and approval as he strives to (1) understand himself and (2) have others take him seriously.
- A parent-constructed profile of her youngster organizes her own thinking, reveals considerable information, and serves as a basis for future comparisons.
- Emotions play an even larger role in learning than previously recognized, but schools are not equipped to address this factor of learning. Emotions are directly related to motivation, without which little learning takes place.
- The thinking mechanisms of adolescents are undergoing transformation as they reexamine their environment in terms of their newly developing cognitive processes.
- Teenagers need some latitude in their attempts to reach an adult-type decision-making capacity but also require help in gaining the experience necessary for mature judgments.
- Parents can and should take advantage of school offerings while improving their child's ability to learn. The knowledge provided by the school, plus the process of learning provided by the parent-directed remedial program, will culminate in higher achievement.

With an understanding of her child in the world of the adolescent, the parent is ready to implement the recommended procedures for raising her student's academic prowess. The goals of the program, enumerated in the first chapter, barring unforeseen elements and conditions, are now attainable.

Wrap-Up

If the conventional remedial measures for reversing scholastic underachievement haven't worked in the past, the parent should not expect them to succeed, somehow, in the present. Rewards, punishment, and lectures have their place, but when they are unsuccessful—and for the chronic underachiever they usually are—the parent should opt for the new methodologies outlined herein. Utilize the methodology suggested in the subsequent chapters.

12

Energizing Cognitive and Affective Structure through Discussion

PARENT ONE: That's too scary. I think I know what you're talking about when I'm reading it, but later I'm not so sure. You talk about the affect and cognition. They're not words I use every day. I've had no training in this field.

PARENT TWO: I'm not distracted by the terminology, but I just don't have time to teach my kid everything you say he should understand. I still think it's the job of the school to educate.

EDUCATIONAL THERAPIST: The points you two have brought up have already been covered, but instructors know that telling is not teaching. Even in graduate classes, I felt it necessary to clarify some material by expressing it a second or third time but in different terms.

PARENT ONE: I'm glad you said "graduate classes." I didn't want you to think I'm not too swift.

THERAPIST: Let's take a quick review of your misgivings. The *affect* is a whole class of mental processes that includes temperament, moods, feelings or emotions. I'm equating it with emotions. *Cognitive* means all the forms of knowing, including perception, imagination, judgment, and reasoning. I'm more or less equating it with thinking. I've de-emphasized the various learning theories and the terms associated with each. You don't need to know these for this program. As for the time involved, you will not find it overwhelming. In most cases, you spend much more time lecturing, repeating yourself, and fretting over your child than the time this prescription requires. As for the schools, they can't meet this obligation at the present time. If they could, your kids probably wouldn't be underachievers.

Learning Readiness

A major problem of adolescence occurs when the learner disassociates the school curriculum from his personal needs. What, he ponders, does geometry have to do with the purpose of life? Why should he study a foreign language if he has no intention of leaving Nebraska? What does English literature have to do with his search for identity? How can history help him make sense out of the confusing world he's living in right now? The culmination of his skepticism about school subjects is the eventual diminution of his effort, which results in lower grades. "So what?" he asks. Marks in school are just as unrelated to the real world as the subjects he's supposed to study are irrelevant to his life. To his teachers and his parents, spoken or implied, he conveys the message: Get real.

You can tell him what you think he ought to know, but remember the caveat: telling isn't teaching. Teaching, or efforts at teaching, will be useless unless actual learning takes place. If he rejects your explanations, openly or silently, you haven't effected a change. The internal mechanisms of the mind already in place must accommodate the new information or ideas in order to assimilate them. He may listen politely, acknowledge your position, and possibly express agreement, but unless his behavior, relative to the topic, is altered, he hasn't grasped what you wanted him to learn. He may have learned that certain actions on his part, or lack of the same, will bring about a punishment. He may, especially in the short term, do whatever is necessary to avoid that penalty. However, he still sees no reason why he should study chemistry.

The parental task is not merely to exercise authority or instruct in specific subjects but to guide the adolescent toward desired goals that will be meaningful to him as an individual. This is a different youngster than he was during his preteens. His thinking and his emotions are on a new level even though he's not aware of the change. Because of his cognitive and affective development, an opportunity has arisen that never existed before. Educators speak of readiness in the young child. The child has to be ready for school, ready to leave his mother for hours, ready to take care of his personal needs, ready to listen, and ready to read. He can't, says the teacher, learn specific study units until he is ready. Readiness is a maturational level for each developmental area.

A new type of readiness, overlooked by educators, now appears as the youngster enters formal operations. He's becoming ready to think and feel as an adult. The opportunity to hone his skills is now evolving. The school can teach him sophisticated subject matter when he's ready. You, the parent, can make him ready to learn whatever the school has to offer.

A Learning Game

Life is a problem-solving activity. A major element in resolving issues is experience, which may be direct or vicarious, or a blend of the two. A single parent or a wife–husband team should use every advantage and every possibility to foster the development of the teenager's advancing thinking potential. One of these learning games, certainly a major one, takes the form of a planned family roundtable. Roundtable discussions should be designed to construct a positive attitude toward learning that could last for a lifetime.

Start by setting up a family meeting. This will be a discussion consisting of all the household members who are able to participate. If you're a single parent with one child, the group will number two. If you and your husband have three adolescent children, then the group will have five participants. The other children need not be underachievers, nor belong to any particular category. If they're living at home, they're qualified.

The purpose of these meetings should be made clear to the participants. Use no subterfuge. They're designed to raise the level of "John's" schoolwork; therefore, say so. Then, set up the guidelines, which may vary from family to family. An adult should preside over the first series of meetings.

- Announce the purpose as stated. We're going to enhance "John's" academic capabilities.
- We're going to have a family meeting for one hour each week at a set time, which is not to be cancelled for frivolous reasons. No one is to miss the meeting. If something arises that makes the meeting time very inconvenient, another time will be selected.
- The meetings will center around preselected topics, and John will choose the first three. The initial topics should be currently on television or appear in newspapers or magazines. There may be some limitation, but most subjects are eligible for review. John may select areas of his personal interest, from football games to TV specials on why students don't like school, to a war somewhere in the world, to a favorite situation comedy.
- Television programs may be watched prior to the meeting or, if a VCR is available, taped earlier and shown at a convenient time. Written material that is to be analyzed should be passed around for perusal to all participants well before the meeting.
- A discussion about the article or television selection should start the meeting. Questions to be asked about the contents under discussion can be applied to other topics of a similar nature. For example, John selects a Sunday morning news

show, one of the "talking heads" variety. They're on every week with a topic the television producer considers timely. People, John feels, are interested in this. The subject is analyzed by each participant in the family meeting:

What is the problem?
Is it stated clearly by the moderator?
Are both sides of a question presented?
Are cogent arguments offered?
Are there contradictions?
Are the facts presented by one side ignored by the other?
Do the program participants display too much emotion instead of sound arguments?
Are their arguments obvious, hackneyed, threadbare?
Do they offer anything new or enlightening?
Are their assumptions based on evidence?
Do any debate by filibustering, interrupting, or shouting?
Does the moderator have a bias?
Does the moderator cut off the microphone hoggers and try for an even-handed approach?
Can the program be summed up as capsulizing the topic and offering constructive suggestions?
Does the listener know any more now than before the program was presented?

The questions herein, of course, are general, and any may be deleted or new ones added, but this is only the beginning. The second phase takes some experience and will become more polished with time. The questions asked and observations made by the roundtable discussants are now pursued in greater depth.

Analyze the moderator and each guest or regular on the program.
Are the guests truly informed or merely expressing some form of ideology?

Are the guests "experts" in the field, qualified through training and/or experience, or are they merely interested parties?
Did any of these participants offer ideas that are worth pursuing?
What inferences might be drawn from the arguments presented, and are any conclusions possible?
What arguments were overlooked?
What additional data should have been offered?
Is there a third side to the views presented?
Who and what influenced the members of the family roundtable?
What are the thoughts of each member of the family?
Is the topic of sufficient interest to discuss it again at a future meeting?

The chairperson in this second phase may be rotated for the meetings to follow. Your teenager, who selected the initial subjects, should be given the occasional opportunity to choose topics again. He may not be interested in a news item, but he's interested in something. Suppose he selects a football game. What should be discussed? You can review the game, but that is of little interest, especially for someone who does not follow football. Try some new approaches. Talk about the broadcasters and their voices, their knowledge, their grammar (e.g., "Just between you and I, the coach made a mistake"), their observational ability, their interpretive capabilities, and the richness of their vocabularies (e.g., "He burst right through, eh and boom! and ugh! Oh my!"). Ask the group to make corrections and to recommend descriptive terms. Encourage John to do so.

Dramas and sitcoms are also easy. Was this program true to life, and was it supposed to be? Can this program tell a tale without incorporating a social message? Are people really like that? Did some character overreact or some person overact? Do people actually speak that way? Why is one program interesting and the other a turnoff?

In this second-level phase of discussion, family members may suggest how the story could be changed or the script improved. Could a particular character have been better portrayed? Should there be a follow-up to this episode, and if so, what might transpire?

The family roundtable game has almost limitless possibilities and should be shaped to fit the individuals involved. Expect some members to become interested in areas they may have disdained earlier. The range of topics may be expanded and eventually include subjects not covered by the media or entertainment shows, such as personal or family problems or individuals known to all.

The rules might be changed with experience to fit general family interest. The time may be altered. One hour is only a starting point. There may be any number of meetings in a given week, and follow-up discussions may become possible. The parent has considerable latitude in organizing and fine-tuning the meetings.

The purpose of this activity is to involve the underachiever in something of interest to him and have him give thought to a topic with the encouragement and opportunity to express his thoughts to others.

Deep involvement over time should erase his emotional misgivings about his identity, his place in society, and his ability to understand issues and express himself. If conducted with sincerity, the talk group will produce surprising and gratifying results. The fact that news or sports or other events may be learned is of secondary importance. The underachiever is learning about himself and constructing areas of interest while he builds his own confidence. You'll know you've hit the jackpot when your John announces, "I've written up the topic for today because it's not in the paper or on television. Today we're going to talk about me!"

Parental Inputs

The game of family discussions offers many benefits and should be pursued as vigorously as the participants and the situation permit. Some cautions are in order, however. As a parent you should:

- Avoid mandating any particular topic, but you may certainly offer suggestions.
- Put aside your own ego and allow your child to burnish his. As an adult, talking with your own children, you don't need credit for predicting something accurately or being right. "I told you so" doesn't fit with this exercise. If one of the participants says, "That's what Mom has been saying all along," merely acknowledge the statement.
- Be careful not to monopolize the conversation, even if you have many unuttered incisive and learned comments in reserve. Say enough to keep the discussion going on the topic and intervene if anyone is becoming argumentative.
- Point out that some problems have no one answer or cannot be settled by the possible solutions available at the time. For example, "Should every identifiable ethnic group in every country be given statehood if it so desires?"
- Stress what an event being discussed means to the family in general and the adolescent in particular.
- Suggest that the adolescent seek other possible solutions, and offer some if no one else does. "Perhaps an alternative to limiting imports is to manufacture better and less expensive products ourselves. How can we do that?"
- Move away from the obvious concrete situation. "Yes, that's right. That's how it plays today. But let's look at it in another light. Suppose we alter some things. What could be changed?"
- Attempt to have the adolescent evaluate the thoughts of others in some fair manner.
- Suggest possible unplanned outcomes when solutions are offered to problems until the adolescent starts to allow for contingencies.
- Note how some unpleasant events could have been prevented with planning and the implementation of a few cau-

tionary steps. The possible consequences of actions should be highlighted.

- Call attention, especially early in the game, to all the possible relationships in the situations under discussion. If the adolescent misses some logical connection between events, the parent may drop a hint or, if necessary, make an assertion. "Maybe the president doesn't want to fire him so soon. He's a presidential appointee. How would such a quick dismissal reflect on the president?"
- Acknowledge errors or shortsightedness in your own thinking. "I never thought of that, John. Maybe I'll have to reconsider."

The Expanding Horizon

The adolescent starts this type of activity, usually, by clinging to familiar topics such as sports, music, or automobiles. As he builds confidence, his horizons broaden and he opens up to exploring new subject matter. Adolescents love to criticize, and, finding that the game not only permits but advocates constructive criticism, he will become more enthused about playing.

Variations of the game keep it fresh and generate the responses desired. For instance, you may play "Pick on the Pundit." You may scrutinize the performances of high-salaried electronic journalists. One participant recently noticed that a familiar correspondent, noted for his abrasiveness, when backed into a corner because of his weak position, raises his voice and speaks quickly. When the situation calls for a retort, he reaches into his sparsely populated repertoire of illuminating responses and verbally assaults his opponents with stunning phrases such as "Horse feathers!" and "Root causes!"

The discussion group, now more advanced, will be more demanding as it continues with the same type of questions and analyses.

These news talk show journalists are usually harsh critics. They ask hard questions of their guests and demand single-sentence answers. They seem to enjoy center stage without guests and often supply their own views and predictions. They, however, are rarely held accountable for their errors. The teenage game allows the adolescent to be the critic, something he can do with ebullience. Who gets criticized? The television journalist and his guest experts.

Some suggested options for playing are as follows:

- Clip written opinions from authorities and reevaluate them after some time has passed. There are an endless number of experts in fields such as sports, politics, sociology, economics, and even the weather. How well do these authorities forecast the pennant winners or the Dow Jones Industrial Average?
- Create a profile of television commentators such as those on Sunday morning news shows. As soon as the subject of the show is revealed, predict the positions of each regular. Have a contest for how many times Journalist A will interrupt the guest trying to respond to a question.
- Decide, after watching, which commentator places the answer in the question and refuses to let the guest say otherwise.
- Search for inconsistencies in positions and note that humans are ever prone to this error.
- Determine which journalists, in effect, attempt to "interview themselves" by dominating the program, even though the guest is a prominent person.
- Decide which commentators hold to biased viewpoints irrespective of changing facts, and discuss only those bits of information that support their position.

Talk shows featuring one or two hosts or hostesses make good family topics. These tend to be shown during the school day, but a taped program can be played on a weekend. The tape has other advantages, also. A statement can be reviewed to determine accuracy. Often, someone will state categorically, "I didn't say that!" A review of the tape can clarify such issues.

The adolescent can play pollster and report his findings about a particular issue at the family meeting. He need not stand in a shopping mall and ask questions of strangers, although this would be permissible. He could limit his queries to a few questions to people he knows, such as friends, neighbors, and relatives. The report he makes will help him think as never before. The trick is to rephrase questions to change the for-and-against percentages in controversies. For example:

Primary question: Should the government provide immediate housing for all the homeless in the United States?

Altered question: Should the government place a $200 surcharge on your taxes to provide immediate housing for all the homeless in the United States?

The news-reporting shows make interesting diagnoses for the teenager examining society and finding his place in it. He can learn to analyze by noting the phraseology used by correspondents. An example may be the number of times unrevealed sources are mentioned to present a picture that may or may not be accurate. He can listen for a standby such as:

"Our network has learned . . ."

"According to an insider . . ."

"A high official revealed . . ."

"Knowledgeable people told us . . ."

"Reliable sources say . . ."

"Unconfirmed reports suggest . . ."

Some of your teenager's observations may resemble those of other adolescents who are pushing their newfound cognizant powers into high gear.

"Notice that the coach said last week that the game was lost because the players didn't play as a team."

"Yes, that's what he said."

"Well, this week they won because of a 'common effort.' "

"Yes. He said that."

"When the team lost, they made some mistakes; they played badly."

"Yes, doesn't that sound reasonable?"

"Something's missing."

"The other team?"

"Sure. Don't they have anything to do with it? Isn't the way they played part of the game? Maybe when our team won, the other team made a lot of mistakes. Maybe when we made a lot of mistakes, the other team forced them? Huh?"

Sports writers sometimes give credit to the playing of the opposition, especially if they have an outstanding player who performed admirably in the game. But it is often reported that the home team played poorly or well without accounting for the opposition.

One parent, after a New York Giants–Philadelphia Eagles football game, bought the New York and Philadelphia newspapers the next day for comparison purposes. Although there was some brief mention of the opposition in each local account, the focus was on the home team. The game was described as if the opponent consisted of mechanical beings who played precisely as programmed with the outcome of each play dependent only on the home team's skill.

The adolescent, faced with the reality and the evidence, begins to think beyond his immediate perceptions. He comes to the realization that the same incident can produce many views and that analyses and conclusions are influenced by emotions. Learning in the human mind is transferrable. The subject at hand may be unimportant, but his enriched process of thinking will be used elsewhere, including school. Learning extends far beyond simply memorizing and repeating knowledge to applying previously mastered knowledge and experiences to new situations.

In some discussions, early on, the adolescent may rush into a quick judgment. "It's wrong. Change it." He may close his thought mechanisms to suggestions of the innumerable problems involved in this "change." The situations, of course, vary, but a very real case came up during one roundtable discussion, which serves as a good example.

The item in question stemmed from a situation revealed by an uncle of "John" the evening before. The uncle was the proprietor of an accounting firm that employed nine people: two secretaries, five accountants with dissimilar experience, and two certified public accountants. One of the latter, Ted, had been with John's uncle for nearly fifteen years and had been a reliable and competent staff member. Each of the previous fourteen years, the uncle had given him and his other employees their annual salary increase. In the current year, the proprietor announced a raise for each worker except Ted.

As expected, Ted requested a meeting and, reasonably enough, asked for an explanation.

TED: I can't understand why I didn't get a raise. Was it something I did? Has my work fallen off?

PROPRIETOR (UNCLE): No, you've done the same responsible work you've always done. I have no complaints about your efforts.

TED: Then why . . .?

PROPRIETOR: I really can't afford to increase my expenses more than I have already. It's my way of starting to limit costs.

TED: But why me? Couldn't you cut everyone else's raise just a fraction and give me the same percentage as the rest of the staff?

PROPRIETOR: Yes, I could but that doesn't solve my problem. Ted, I'm paying you too much right now. I've thought about it for a long time. I'm freezing your salary.

TED: You mean I won't get a raise next year either?

PROPRIETOR: Probably not.

TED: I can't see how you figure. Everybody gets raises every year. If I'm a good employee, why not?

PROPRIETOR: This is not easy. Look. This is a small firm. On your side, you do your work and you've been here for a long time.

TED: And that doesn't mean anything?

PROPRIETOR: It means that I'm keeping you on the payroll. But look at my side. You've done good work but I paid you well all those years.

TED: Yes, but . . .

PROPRIETOR: Hold on. Let's face facts. I can replace you immediately with a CPA at only sixty percent of what you're making now. That means the other forty percent is coming out of my pocket. This isn't General Motors. I'm getting older. I want to stash some money away. But look, I'm not cutting your salary and I'm not letting you go. What I've decided to do is not increase your take any more until your salary is level with the market.

Ted went on to present the argument that his personal contributions to the firm were unrelated to the going rate for accountants. He had, he insisted, helped to build the business over the years, and if he were paid more than the others in his position, that was his reward for helping to put the company on firm ground. He wasn't, he stated, asking for too much or even anything special. He just wanted the same percentage raise as everyone else. He had been loyal for almost fifteen years and he was owed loyalty in return.

"He's right. Ted's right," exclaimed John. "Uncle is dead wrong. He's making plenty of money. He should share it with a guy who's been there a long time."

The roundtable participants were split on the question of equity, justification, and moral rights. This type of imbroglio is just what the educational doctor calls for to get the teenager actively involved in thinking and feeling. In this particular case, the youngster changed his mind the second time the topic came up for discussion. He had looked at other possibilities besides a raise or no-raise issue, considered a bonus plan based on the net income of the business, and the possibility of an increase in benefits in lieu of raises. Finally, he sided with his uncle. Your teenager may decide otherwise. His decision and yours might differ. You want him to consider all of the facts available, including the worker's and the proprietor's views, the economics, the obligations implied, the question of justice, if it applies, and solutions other than those offered by the proprietor and the worker.

The Roundtable Goes Round and Round

There are instances when a parent would like to see the conclusions reached by her youngster conform to her own thinking. Ethical values would certainly be an example. The use of illegal drugs, alcohol, and dangerous acts are others. These discussions afford an opportunity to get facts on the table for examination and share opinions for analyses.

You can express your ideas in this forum without lecturing, shouting, or threatening. Discuss them. Remember that telling is not enough. Ideally, you want your teenager to reach the "right" conclusions himself in these threatening issues. If your child already agrees with you, avoid the subject other than a mention in passing. Notice that in Sample A of the profiles in Chapter 3, the mother happily reported that her daughter could not be persuaded by peers to use drugs. When the adolescent is undecided, you have the odds on your side. If your child is on the other side of the fence, your task is obviously more difficult, but not impossible.

"School is all right but it's just not as important as you think. If, when the time comes, I need the grades, I'll get them." Parent, if you hear something like this, make a mental note to discuss careers, job satisfaction, and earnings. There has been a one-word change over the years as teenagers recognize the importance of a career and training:

1960s: "Make love not money."

1990s: "Make love and money."

Various alternatives are available to get points across in discussions while keeping your offspring interested:

- Play devil's advocate. Be sure he knows what it means, that is, that you are advocating something you may not believe in just for the sake of argument. Since you are "playing" at opposing, you can get away with much that otherwise might offend him.
- Have him play devil's advocate after he sees how it's done. Be sure *you're* not easily offended.
- Have your teenager play the role of someone other than himself to try "walking in that person's shoes." He may, for example, be a prisoner in an overcrowded institution making "reasonable" humanitarian requests.
- Have him compare short-term and long-term solutions to problems. How do they differ, and does the use of one cancel out the effectiveness of the other? What would he offer?
- Expose him to irrational or irrelevant arguments, but give him the chance to understand, consider, and respond. Use "nonsequitor thinking" instead of logic—"So you now think Ted shouldn't get a raise, so I suppose you're against all unions."
- Play courtroom. He can be the plaintiff's or defendant's attorney or the jury. Here are the facts. Ted's attorney claims an implied contract between Ted and the proprietor that was confirmed by yearly raises over a fourteen-year period.

An Unfolding Vision

The discussions may be filled with humor or be of a serious nature. The prime purpose is to provide an opportunity for the youngster to think, to express his thoughts, to evaluate the validity of his thoughts, and to examine his own feelings. He will certainly learn much about subjects he considers nonacademic, but he'll come to realize that many of the disciplines taught in school are not isolated and limited to formal education but are a part of worldly events. For instance, current incidents are a result of historical occurrences, science is intertwined with everyday living, and Shakespeare may have been the most insightful psychologist who ever wrote. As John said, "You know, Mom, I think some of the things they (the school) teach us *are* relevant." His mother had been trying to present this belief for a year without success. He had to discover it himself.

As he discusses written and televised events and stories, he'll start to relate his personal being with his environment. He'll be clarifying his identity and his relationships. The reading and watching with a purpose in mind and the subsequent analysis will expand his neighborhood. Through practice, he'll learn to screen the massive stimuli and categorize, accept, and reject elements through his own mental screening process. He'll see other people's failures, problems, successes, and values and his own place in a new era which some call postmodernism. This is his world. He'll understand the nature of instant global communication, progress, and opportunity at a time begging for the services of an achiever.

Wrap-Up

The underachieving teenager must discover learning and its fruits for himself. Telling him about it is insufficient. You, as a parent, can help make this self-discovery possible.

The family roundtable is an ideal forum for mental nutrition. Each parent must decide herself when this should be scheduled, its specific provisions, and the rules to enforce it.

Participants in the roundtable may also be aunts, uncles, and grandparents. Too many people will dilute the effort, but alternating participants is acceptable.

The discussions should begin at a preset time and end before interest begins to wane. The principle used by stand-up comedians —to always leave them laughing—may be utilized in terms of discontinuing the talk while people still have much to say. Use a television technique—"To be continued."

Most parents will be surprised at how much they, themselves, will learn. This is a plus since their enthusiasm will be contagious. Be sure to initiate the program with a subject of interest to your adolescent. If he could have any car he wanted when he's eligible to drive, which one would he choose and why?

Although the initial topics should be about areas interesting to your adolescent and chosen by him, later topics may be chosen by other participants. Community, national, and world events are usually appropriate, as well as are general social, scientific, sporting, and health subjects. A particular theme may be repeated so long as interest remains. For example, during the period of political campaigns, it is likely that the issues, the personalities, and the qualifications of the candidates could be reviewed at length.

As your youngster becomes more adept at analyzing the questions under consideration, you can interject the content of this work at planned intervals. For instance, your teenager might find it interesting to discuss adolescence, its pleasures and problems, and, certainly, the thirteen-year-old (or whatever age he is) in school. Center the discussions around whatever he considers relevant.

Return to your profile of the youngster. Make whatever modifications are necessary and then look for his weaknesses in learning. Determine his needs and then schedule the specific areas as topics for the roundtable. If he has, say, extreme difficulty in bouncing back after stumbling, hold a discussion in which each participant reveals mistakes and failures in his own life. Talk about how these were or might have been overcome. Reread the section on setbacks (Chapter 15) and present appropriate material to the group.

Do the same at different sessions for each area of weakness. Give your teenager the opportunity to understand that all humans have failings, that problems are common to all, and that success in life depends on the individual's ability to adjust and to try again.

Be sure to schedule the topics covered in this work that are essential for academic success. Some that lend themselves to discussion focus on:

- The causes and effects of procrastination.
- The importance of homework.
- The desirability of flexibility.
- The value of analytical listening.
- The usefulness of self-reliance.
- The consequences of decisions and actions.
- The necessity for a skilled plan of attack for challenging tasks.

Chapter Footnote: Ted went to John's uncle five weeks after their discussion and gave notice. He accepted a position in a large company at a substantially lower salary but with excellent possibilities of increases and promotions.

13

Communicating—Adult Style

Listening

"She doesn't listen," complained the distraught mother. "No matter what I say, she turns it off. How do I break through?"

"There's an old joke about hitting a donkey over the head with a board just to get his attention—but you can't do that. However, you must get her attention." The educator paused to think. "You can borrow some of the strategies used by advertisers for your daughter."

The reader can do likewise. First, decide on your priorities. If you have adopted the family roundtable discussion format, you may deem it advisable to wait until the next meeting before bringing up a subject for analysis. You may decide the topic can't wait. It should be done now. The general rule is to get her attention. But how?

Newspapers learned the use of headlines to attract people's attention. "TRANSPORTATION STRIKE IMMINENT!" in large bold letters would capture the attention of people heading for subways or bus stops. The supermarket tabloids never worry about how outlandish attention grabbers are as long as some customers give in to their curiosity. "WOMAN, 73, HAS MARTIAN-

FATHERED TWINS!" Television shows start with clips of the story to be shown after the introduction and six or seven commercials. Stay tuned. Even the news programs, finishing one report, will highlight the next one coming up right after the break. If you want people to be interested, get their attention.

Each parent must decide on her own strategy to fit her unique problem. Try opening the conversation with something the audience, in this case your child, is sure to welcome. The typical adolescent, when you wish to present a topic and she is in a hurry, will respond with something like, "What are you going to tell me I haven't heard a hundred times before?" Fool her.

"Your father and I were considering raising your allowance."

"I decided that you don't have to baby-sit your brother this Saturday night. You're free to go out with your friends."

"Maybe you are right. Maybe you should have a new outfit for that dance."

"Dad wanted me to tell you that it's all right. You can go to the concert."

You've grabbed her attention and she's listening. Don't spoil it with a long harangue on the necessity of doing her homework. Another one liner will do. Throw in your condition as a given sans discussion. "Of course, we assume that all of your school assignments will be completed to date."

One teenager liked the inducement but not the condition and stopped to present her position. Her mother interrupted with, "What excuses are you going to offer I haven't heard a hundred times before?"

Give-and-take, accommodation, conciliation, and compromise are all good topics for roundtable discussions. You've offered something in return for something. Note that rebuttals are acceptable, but she'll have to wait for the next family conference to present it. Meanwhile, she will have time to consider her attitude. In her stage of development, she can draw inferences, see possibilities, and think about her own actions and her own feelings. That's precisely what you want her to do. She may not be compliant initially, but, with time, she'll come to understand where her interests lie.

The listening process may be brief or quite lengthy. In the classroom the student may have forty minutes to focus on a teacher's lecture. Most teachers will break up the period into several activities to allow for the probable attention span of the class members. Nevertheless, listening, for whatever length of time, is a skill. The family meetings can serve to sharpen this ability.

Exchanging Messages

Just as telling isn't necessarily teaching, talking may not qualify as communication. A student may appear to read well in class, with the correct inflections, pauses, modulation, and pronunciation, but not possess an adequate comprehension of the material read. The listener, too, must understand the speaker's message or communication breaks down. Why wouldn't the listener decipher and digest spoken words? As with many explanations of human behavior, the answer is multifold. Consider a student listener in a school auditorium. She:

- Has thrown her audio-off switch. She is not receptive to the points offered, has heard it too often before, and is just not interested.
- Doesn't understand the message; it is unclear, too subtle, too complex, or the vocabulary being used is unfamiliar.
- Has other topics on her mind. Her thoughts are elsewhere, perhaps on an exciting weekend approaching or a test she fears taking.
- Is too tired or ill to be receptive to almost anything. She just wants to be free of this ordeal, that is, confined to an immovable seat with only her thoughts as a means of escape.
- Is distracted by being attracted to a boy within sight or a friend using motions to send a silent message.

- Is taking advantage of this opportunity to do some homework due the next period. Time is running out.

Some Rules of the Game

Some of the same interferences to listening apply to casual conversations and the family roundtable format. As a parent, however, you have an advantage in this setting. You want your child to be attentive or the time is wasted. You, therefore, should follow some general guidelines.

The subject matter early in the game must center around the adolescent's interests. That's why she should select the topic in the initial conferences.

When the teenager speaks, you and all of the members of the group must listen. Feigned attention will only discourage her.

Uninterrupted, overemotional discourses by the adolescent or anyone else should be halted by raising a question. Instead of "No, no. You've missed the essentials of this whole thing," try "Wait a second. I'm having difficulty following your line of reasoning. Is this what you're saying . . .?" You might know exactly what she means, but belittling her will be counterproductive. You want her to talk. Asking for clarification shows you're attentive and interested. Such a tactic creates a pause, which may help her reconsider her position. The meaning of her words, repeated or rephrased, might be altered considerably. You've set aside the initial words she's uttered, which may have been too emotionally oriented, and given her that necessary moment for reflection. That's your aim at these meetings: to increase cognition and decrease emotion.

If you wish to interject a remark, you need not always ask for clarification. By a prearranged rule, you should halt the speaker by raising a finger and allowing the person talking to complete a sentence or even an entire thought. All members of the group should abide by the same procedure, which you may refer to as Conference Courtesy. In the previous chapter, the recommendation was made to use the news talk shows to illustrate how rudeness or mike hogging is used to cover weak arguments, prevent an adversary from presenting strong arguments, or simply for ego polishing. Your family conference participants, once you've laughed at the professionals, will not wish to emulate them.

You should avoid discouraging your child from participating, even if you totally disagree with whatever she advocates. Without yielding substantive points, you can deflect undesirable positions by your wording.

"Let's see. I understand your position. It's not the same as mine so I'll have to weigh your arguments very carefully. Let's review this again next time and see if we can reach some agreement. In the meantime, give some thought to what I've been saying. Maybe you can find some merit in my argument."

"You are really growing up. That is not a childish challenge you offered. I'm not at all sure you're right this time but you've given me something to consider."

Flaws

Listening skills may be taught by offering general examples. Have the listener become aware of the difficulties involved in communicating so that she will recognize the warning signs when she senses them. Review real situations, based on personal experiences, when good attention became difficult. Sitting in an audience, described above, is one illustration. Unless the speaker's words have meaning for members of the audience, communication, of course, is nonexistent. The other illustrations can revolve around two or several people having what may be loosely termed a "conversation." One person may be trying to explain a view while the supposed listener is impatiently waiting for her to finish. A bystander might read the mind of the supposed listener—"If only she would shut up, I'll tell her how it really works." In other instances, some naturally gregarious people or compulsive talkers monopolize the conversation while the supposed listener gazes about the room with telltale glazed eyes. There is, also, the agreeable but annoying listener who improves on anything the speaker says.

"It's the best seafood restaurant from New York to the Mississippi."

". . . from New York to California!"

"Hundreds of people would have done likewise."

"Thousands . . . !"

Finally, there is the listener who will always outdo the speaker.

"Can you imagine. There I was, a witness to a three-car accident."

"Let me tell you about the time I witnessed a seven-car pileup."

The listeners in these latter examples feel compelled to project themselves into the focus of the conversation. They concentrate on possible openings for this projection and, in so doing, easily miss interesting and important accounts offered by the speaker. The communicative process is thereby impaired.

Practice

After discussing these and other impediments to effective listening and the resulting weakening of communication, the parent should then explain how to strengthen listening skills. The answer is practice. Simply practice listening.

Listen to a radio program or to a television speech. Have several people take notes, and then compare them. Transfer this technique to all forms of communication.

What was said?
What appeared to be new?
What was important?
Was anything unclear?
How might the presentation have been improved?

Did the speaker do what she said she was going to do?

A student's skills can be enhanced greatly by taping a televised speech or dialogue—preferably a short one—viewing it a second time, and transcribing it so that it may be read afterwards. A message in writing is subject to careful analysis. The speaker, with facial expressions, gesticulating hands, and voice inflections, can give his words a substance that may be illusionary. Reduced to black and white, phrases stand on their own merit and can be evaluated objectively. Errors, redundancies, and weak justifications, concealed by a skilled speaker's mannerisms, are now exposed.

Parents usually find it relatively easy to involve youngsters in games of listening, analysis, and evaluation, especially of television personalities. Adolescents find a great satisfaction in criticizing in general and the establishment in particular. Are you then creating an unreasonable and always dissatisfied critic? The answer seems obvious if the criticism is directed at talk show hosts, announcers, journalists, or other television people who are well compensated and portray themselves as experts. If they err, and they do frequently, if they are unprepared for the topic, which is not unusual, if they specialize in criticizing others, and they generally do, and if they want to be in the position they're in, and of course they do, then they should be fair game. However, an innocent person, for example a witness to an accident, facing a television camera should not be subjected to the same judgmental criteria. Your teenager should understand the difference.

Listening carefully to television programs develops a transferable skill which will affect your child's:

1. Self-esteem and confidence.
2. Ability to receive, screen, process, and evaluate information from many sources.
3. Capability to raise her academic performance in high school and college.
4. Insight into the thoughts and motivations of others.
5. Efforts to improve social relationships over a lifetime.

6. Ability to bond with you, her parents, almost immediately and in the coming years.

Relationships

Anyone working closely with teenagers is aware of their penchant for criticism of school, established institutions, societal attitudes, and—their favorite target—their parents. Then, in their late teens and twenties, they realize that Mom wasn't such a fool after all. Comedians usually can create a joke or two about the late teenager who is surprised at how much his parents have learned in the past few years. In reality, the young adult has assembled his free-floating thoughts, gained some personal experience, and matured in an intellectual sense. Much remains to be learned, but his mental structural organization has been completed. He can now think as an adult.

"I remember as I approached adolescence how I resented the restrictions my mother imposed on my brothers and me. We had to be in the house by dark, or on time for dinner even when it was still daylight, and off to bed before we were tired. Each of us had household chores. Some we did all the time; I did the dishes. Other responsibilities were related, such as making sandwiches for everyone for the next day's lunch at school. Mom was inflexible. If you were supposed to do something, you had to do it. There was no way out.

"Now I look back and wonder how she did as much as she did. Dad was in the army, a professional soldier. There were four of us kids and Mom had no help, not even a grandparent to relieve her once in a while. She was strict all right but we had a good home. She was always there for us no matter what the problem. I didn't know it then, but it was a home full of love, and there were a lot of nice ritual-type events. Dad would come home Saturday for the weekend, and all four of us were allowed to go to the movies. As a matter of fact, we had to go.

"I guess she deserves a hell of a lot of credit. We all turned out all right. But back then, at twelve, I saw things differently. Twenty years and being the mother of two certainly changes your viewpoint. Mom was really a great girl and those restrictions weren't so bad!"

Parental Relationship

Viewpoints undergo constant transformation as the mentally maturing youngster slowly reduces his dependence on parents, but the visible conflicts distort the true strength of the connection beneath the surface. This is the time of their lives when they are looking around and asking questions, developing a healthy skepticism, and challenging different elements in their environment. They are examining themselves as well as others and are not at all as certain as their behavior indicates.

Parents are still, and will remain for a few more years, the major influence over the young adolescent. Children at this stage will try to relate to their parents; only some will succeed. The adult must leave the door open, and condescending statements can sometimes slam it shut.

"You know, John, you can talk to me at any time about any subject. I'll be glad to help."

This approach is fine for preadolescent children, but this juvenile is rapidly developing his own mind. John, in his new mental era, is likely to respond to such an invitation with an oral acceptance but think, according to his personal values, disrespectful thoughts.

"What do you know? You're only interested in Meg (sister)."

"Sure. Talk to you. You can't solve your own problems."

"Since when have you learned to listen? You never did before."

A good relationship with your offspring will not be established by impromptu expressions of concern. The words must be pointed and sincere but, above all else, accompanied by actions. If you have established a family roundtable with discussions of interest to the teenager, then the initial necessary steps have been taken. If, in this process, you have helped reinforce the need for careful listening and analysis of that input, then you have set the stage for improved family relationships. Remember that the roundtable conference may take forms other than the one recommended—such as dinnertime discussions—but avoid "conferences-on-the-run" and meetings suffering from severe time constraints.

The formal, planned roundtable should not overshadow all other talks with the adolescent. Some things can't wait, or sometimes your child may be open to unusual frankness. A meeting of opportunity is not only permissible but desirable. Not only should you respond to your teenager's request for a talk, but there are times when you don't especially want to wait for a scheduled get-together. Suppose, for instance, that you know John has a social studies project due in two days. He hasn't so much as started the assignment and is now heading for a friend's house for activities other than schoolwork. This may not be the time for a full discussion, but you should put him on notice that he is shirking his responsibility. Give him a reminder that you expect him to meet his obligations.

When you do discuss school try to follow, as far as it is suitable, some guidelines designed to bring about favorable results. This list of "Do's" and "Avoids" will help your conferences reach successful conclusions:

1. Get his attention (no boards over the head).
2. Keep your voice as normal as possible. If it has an edge to it, he'll be placed on guard. You're trying to relate, not dictate.
3. Be clear, brief, and on target. Don't tell any stories, especially about when you were his age.
4. Avoid comparing him with other siblings. Remember this basic psychological fact: he is unique.

5. Avoid excusing him from his obligations. No one else will.
6. Avoid berating him, even if he deserves it. The act of scolding yields little good and tends to make him defensive.
7. Avoid blaming others for his lack of performance, even if you think that they are responsible. He's old enough to shake off peer experiences if he so desires.
8. Let him talk and you listen. All the rules of the listening technique are applicable to you, too.
9. Examine one element of the topic at a time and avoid confusing issues.
10. Avoid all forms of sarcasm, even if you have some good zingers ready to fly. Satisfy your own ego some other way.
11. Steer the conversation toward a relevant course. Main issues must be faced first.
12. Concentrate on the immediate concerns first but refer to future issues.
13. Reveal your parental expectations as if he, of course, will consider them.
14. Avoid asking him to do the work *for you* and get good grades *for you.* Instead, have him aim to perform well *for himself.*
15. Ask for his suggestions about how you or others might help. Promise only what you can deliver.
16. Review precise goals for the effort and be sure that they are attainable.
17. Make it clear that you will respect his privacy. His problems, his efforts, and his strategies are all confidential. Be sure they stay that way.

The parent–teenager relationship is constantly evolving, even if the parent resists. The teenage child remains a child only in terms of being your physical offspring. He is no longer a child in chronological terms. He is venturing cautiously into adulthood but reverts when his need for security is perceived to be threatened. As the months pass, he leans more and more toward the grown-up side. When he finally feels safe with his independence and concomitant responsibility, he severs the apron strings, but the parental bond, composed of love, understanding, and respect, is capable of enduring for life.

These years of eleven or twelve to sixteen are not the final opportunity for you to help your child but are your last chance to assist him in drawing the road map he'll be following for life. Note that a parent "helps." You can't do it for him, but the help can be quite bounteous.

The parent–teenager relationship is constructed largely on the sophisticated skill of listening, but as an intelligent adult, not as an immature child. Both you and your child must master the same skills covered earlier—specifically trying to concentrate on the speaker's words. Now, however, after the conferences, you will understand more than what the words imply by themselves. You might grasp far more than the speaker wishes to reveal. Listening now means becoming aware of implications, of possible exaggerations or lies, of opinions stated as facts, of superficial knowledge of a subject, or of someone forcing arguments into preexisting ideological molds. With your new analytical skills, both you and your student can now determine how a person really feels about the subject he is addressing. Very often and very importantly, this knowledge can help a student anticipate test questions, help an applicant supply the information an interviewer seeks, and help an employee provide the kind of service his boss recognizes and rewards.

Listening: Beyond School

The family roundtable game, then, is played under formal, preset conditions and then extended throughout the parent–child relationship. Adults can also benefit from clear communication, but that is not the purpose of this work.

However, a good example is difficult to reject, especially when the importance of the concept is so clearly illustrated as in the following story.

Recently, a divorceé accepted a dinner date that she had declined several times before. The man in question worked in her building, was eligible, and seemed nice enough but held little attraction for her. He just, she felt, wasn't her type. She graciously refused his very polite requests until four o'clock one afternoon, when weary after an especially difficult day, she met him in the hallway.

"Hi, Doris. Say, I was wondering, if you have no other plans . . ."

"Okay, Brad," she stated as if this were a frequent happening. Doris kept on walking and then, turning her head to the completely nonplussed suitor, added, "Pick me up at seven."

At twelve thirty-three the next morning, Doris gently woke up her mother.

The semi-awake older woman rubbed her eyes trying to focus on Doris's face. Yes, her daughter was smiling. The evening must have gone well.

"Mom," said Doris excitedly. "He listens."

When Are You Successful?

"Instant success" is known to occur after long and laborious effort. The results of your labor may not be apparent immediately. The Greenways were trying to inspire their daughter to raise her academic levels of performance. Kim always seemed to pay attention to the advice her mother and father offered but rarely did anything about it. She was, she announced, a solid C student. Her intelligence tests, her parents protested, placed her in the superior intellectual group. She was, all verified, a classic chronic underachiever.

Kim, now fifteen, seemed well enough adjusted and accepted her role as an underachiever. She also accepted her parents' punishment of her without protest. One evening, speaking on the phone to a friend, she explained, "No, Lisa, I can't go with you

Friday night. No. I can't go Saturday either. That's right. I'm grounded both nights. Well, yeah, the science project. I turned in what I had. Really wasn't good. Mrs. Lodden gave me a D. No. It wasn't worth any more. Sunday? Give me a call. I'll see what I can do."

The Greenways were sitting down at the dining room table with their two children and Mrs. Greenway's parents for the start of their family roundtable. This was to be the fifth session, which was scheduled for every Sunday at one o'clock. Kim seemed to go along with the meetings, although certainly without any great enthusiasm. As they prepared to start, the phone rang. Kim jumped up with an "I'll get it," flew to the kitchen, and said "Hello," all, seemingly, in one second.

"Hi, Lisa. No, I remember. I'll ask them."

"Mom, Lisa wants me to go to the mall with her."

Mrs. Greenway looked at her husband, who, whenever he wished to escape making a decision, tilted his head upward and inspected the ceiling.

"All right, Kim," she said after a moment. "You've been in long enough. Go ahead."

Kim now hesitated. She looked at the phone as if she could see Lisa. "Look, Lisa, my mother says I can go but I don't think she really wants me to. We have this family get-together and all. You know how parents are. I'll see you tomorrow, all right?"

Kim returned to the dining room table and took her place as if Alexander Graham Bell had never lived.

"All right," Kim announced with unusual enthusiasm. "I'm chairing this meeting. Today we're going to talk about fashions, right? Let's get started."

Wrap-Up

Adult-type listening to another person should not be passive. The listener should be actively engaged in interpreting the incoming audio stimuli. What does it mean? What might it mean? What should be added? What is the obvious message of the speaker? Is there a hidden message? What does the obvious or the implied message have to do with me? Is there something I should do in response?

Listening, in its broadest sense, encompasses reading. A person hears, in his mind, his own voice expressing the thoughts of others. The same analytical skills applied to hearing someone speak are applicable to speaking or writing. Instead of asking questions of the speaker, a person should be asking them of himself. Am I saying, or writing, what I want to communicate? Am I saying it directly or implying it? How do I feel about what I'm writing?

All the changing qualities of the adolescent's mental structures, cognitive and affective, are involved in communication. The adolescent must feel that the parent is reliable, interested, and trustworthy before becoming part of the family team. The parent needn't always be right and should be willing to acknowledge and reconsider erroneous decisions.

Discussions may cover many topics, but almost all will, at some instance, tie in with school. The adolescent is concerned about his future, although he may dismiss any talk of it. Plant the seed that scholastic achievement leads to a more successful and happier life, and it will sprout. He needs the respect of family members to develop a healthy self-respect and the confidence necessary to do well in school.

All people are now under the influence, to some measurable degree, of the media. Your child should learn that a proposition stated on television is not irrefutable but is subject to challenge. He should also come to realize that people he sees on the screen may misspeak, twist logic, and err in presenting facts. He, too, should not quit because he isn't perfect; that's the way people are made. His self-image need not be damaged by a faux pas he may commit. He, too, can join the game the world is playing. He is a part of the world; he is a contributing member of the family and of society.

14

Teaching the Art of Learning

"Can you repair an automobile engine?" I asked the distraught mother.

The woman's eyes revealed suspicion. The question was irrelevant. We were discussing her son, whose performance in school was substantially below expectations. What had that to do with car motors?

She responded slowly, deliberately, expecting a trap somewhere. "I couldn't do a very good job nor would I want to."

"But you told me earlier Bill had inherited his mechanical aptitude from you since your husband was decidedly weak in this area."

"Yes. I didn't say positively that he got it from me, but it seems likely. I'm not an expert in Mendelian laws." She then added the word "either."

"But you have the inherent ability. So why can't you repair engines?"

Visibly annoyed, she sputtered, "Because I don't have the interest! Because I wasn't trained in automotive mechanics!"

Bill's mother glared at me. "Can we get on to discussing Bill's work in school?"

"We just did," I replied softly. "Look at what the record reveals.

"His performance is about average for the population as a whole but his innate ability as measured by tests indicates that he should be an A or at least a B student. Now, let's look more closely. In subjects requiring manual dexterity and athletic skill he does well on a consistent basis. In subjects requiring expressions of concepts, his work level drops. Yet, ability tests show he should be good at concept formation.

"Conclusion. Somewhere along the line he has failed to master skills in working out and presenting material he is perfectly capable of mastering."

The suspicion and anger of the parent was rapidly losing ground to an infusion of interest.

"His records point to this explanation of his difficulties. If he had been doing well in school up to a recent point and then fell off or if he is one of those on-and-off students, we would have to look elsewhere for a solution. But notice that despite success in the primary grades, he began to lose ground as he progressed. By the time he reached secondary school, he earned his underachievement label."

Bill's mother's face registered a question before she put it into words. "What has auto repairs to do with this?"

"I was just setting the background for my observation. You made it for me. You weren't trained and you had no particular interest so you couldn't do it. Your interest is more important than your native ability in this area."

"I see. You're saying Bill wasn't offered training in presenting his ideas—in an acceptable fashion."

Now I hesitated. "I'm sure Bill was in attendance when this type of learning was presented, but he missed some essential elements. He does do the work. He just doesn't do it as well as he should. Students who pass don't attract much attention, even though they fail to reach their own potential."

"Add some weaknesses in learning methodology with a lack of interest and we've probably identified the causes of the problem. Without an interest in a subject, the enthusiasm of learners is curtailed. Their product usually reflects this lack, although some students manage to do well in subjects they don't really care about. However, these students have a general interest that overrides any specific negative."

"Where do we go from here?" the parent asked.

"Back to basics. We . . . correction. *You* give him what he needs at home."

"Is a tutor called for?"

"Maybe. First determine his needs."

Individualized Learning Systems

By their teen years, students should have developed learning techniques suitable for themselves that have been tried, modified, and proven effective. Some high schoolers have become very proficient at preparing reports and other projects, digesting usable academic information, and applying that knowledge to other situations as required. These youngsters tend to work at their expected levels and do it without undue strain or time commitments. They're usually designated simply as good students or, if they're substantially above their expected performance, as overachievers. They, themselves, are not aware of utilizing efficient and effective systems to learn. They employ tactics that work for them based on favorable experiences. They may periodically face some very challenging tasks, some setbacks, and some stress. That's part of learning and developing. They do not have the problem, however, of not knowing how to learn. They've progressed beyond that fundamental.

Some students, such as Bill, are faced with the problem of *how*. They lack adequate procedures to prepare the material in a fashion suitable for learning. Consequently, they may allot more time to it than is necessary, employ more energy, and reap more unsatisfactory results.

The parent who helped her child master techniques of doing homework in the elementary grades will not likely be faced with the same problem today. She might still have an underachieving offspring, but the cause will not lie with poor study habits but elsewhere. Is it then too late for the parent who was not sufficiently involved earlier? The answer in most cases is "No, it's not too late but more involved." The younger the child, the more apt he is to follow parental directions. However, new thinking in human development espouses the view that adolescents are more influenced and want to be more cooperative than hitherto suspected. Make your intentions known.

Home Assignments

Scholastic work to be completed outside of school, like Caesar's version of Gaul, is divided into three parts. The most common is assigned by the teacher to be done by the student in a specified manner by a specific date. When homework is mentioned, this type is the one that instantly comes to mind.

A second category of assignment is suggested by the teacher on a voluntary basis. This may be referred to as extra credit and is the favorite of students. Those youngsters striving for grades see this as a way to boost their averages or make up for some lesser omission in the past. It's popular, obviously, because those students satisfied with the status quo don't have to do it. Many of the teen underachievers ignore it. Whatever it is, it doesn't concern them.

The third category is not usually recognized by most students as an assignment. This is additional work on the topic done by the student for the purposes of broadening his knowledge and satisfying his interest. It may consist of an original experiment or an expansion of an experiment done in class. Usually, however, it means suggested but unassigned reading on the subject and, sometimes, informal discussion groups by a few students in the class.

The teacher has, in these cases, titillated at least some of the students who, because of their spiraling interest, want to know more. This is one of the many successes of a good teacher that goes unrecognized and unrewarded. Surprisingly, on occasion, an underachieving student may be found deeply involved in one of these high-interest groups. Here, without being graded, without being tested, and without a deadline to meet, he satisfies his curiosity. One of those kids who despises homework and never volunteers may be deeply immersed in some topic he seems to abhor at school.

The Parent–Consultant

In the primary grades, most parents have little difficulty with subject content. The average adult can readily review and master the work assigned to an eight-year-old. As the child climbs the grades, the challenge to parents increases. By high school, most parents back away from claiming expertise in such areas as algebra, chemistry, physics, and English literature.

A common refrain is, "I did know that at your age, but I haven't used it for years. I can't help without a thorough review." Few wish to review. The common statement is both correct and erroneous. Adults can't be expected to return to high school and relearn or learn for the first time subjects that have no direct bearing on their current lives. However, they can still play an important role in helping their children to learn.

As suggested, some students do well in subjects they do not find interesting. These students have an established system of learning that they employ in all topics, which has become a habit. They utilize these learning skills to achieve success in most areas, which, in turn, creates a momentum that carries over to other classes. The parent of the underachiever helps by fostering an interest whenever possible at the roundtable (Chapter 12), helping the youngster sharpen his listening skills (Chapter 13), and providing an opportunity for the student to improve his scholastic attack skills (later in this chapter).

No one, obviously, knows every subject. Even skilled people frequently have difficulty keeping up with expanding knowledge in their own fields. But expertise in a discipline is not necessary in determining if a student is learning.

A few years ago, an educator applying for a high school principalship was being interviewed by the superintendent of schools and his assistants. After a few personal and innocuous questions, the group began to query seriously. The interviewee was prepared for a barrage of technical questions and was not disappointed. He knew and answered questions about state school law and local school board regulations. He demonstrated familiarity with the rights of students, parents, teachers, and administrators. He was conversant with safety codes and the tedious but important paperwork to be processed. He answered hypothetical questions such as, "What would you do if a painter fell off a scaffold in front of the outside steps one minute before the exit bell?" and "What would you do if the heating system ceased to operate at 11 A.M. on a cold January day?"

Satisfied with his responses to crises management events, the interviewers turned to supervisory duties.

For the first time, because of a moment's pause, the applicant sensed something unusual was coming, perhaps a tricky question. He was correct.

The superintendent sat back in his chair and looked away from the interviewee as if he were formulating a question, but the applicant suspected the district leader already knew exactly the question he wished to pose. "Do you speak Spanish?"

The would-be principal understood that familiarity with Spanish was not a job criterion. "Yes, I do, but certainly not as one who learned the language in childhood. I have a heavy accent but I can communicate."

The school leader nodded his approval. "Do you speak French?"

"No. I know a few common expressions but I definitely do not speak the language."

"Then tell me, sir, how you would evaluate a teacher's instruction in a French class? Suppose your department chairman didn't know French. Suppose there was no one on your faculty who could help. What would you do?"

The question isn't so bad, thought the applicant. In fact, it is rather easy.

"I would evaluate the teacher the same way I would rate every other teacher. I don't have to know biology or electrical repair to evaluate the teachers of these subjects. The evaluative criteria are the same."

The answer satisfied the interviewing group, and some months later the applicant was appointed to the position of high school principal.

A supervisor or administrator can know if children are learning even though, as educators, they don't know the subject matter in question. They can ascertain, sometimes very quickly, a "learning ambience" by (1) the interest of the students, (2) what they are doing, (3) the expressions on their faces, (4) their attention, and (5) their participation. Tests may measure progress objectively, but good instruction or poor teaching can be determined readily by observation.

Evaluative systems are not limited to educators. The same underlying principles frequently apply to diverse enterprises. A restaurateur once explained his decision-making process before adding a new dish to his menu. "First, I put the new item out as a special at a reduced price. Some people try it because it's different and some like the savings."

"You then ask them what they think and then act accordingly," I interjected. Having been consulted as a frequent patron to many local restaurants, I felt qualified to answer for him.

"Right, yes, but wrong. I do ask some people for their opinions, but I don't necessarily go by what they say. Some people like to brag about their knowledge, and some are polite and always say 'fine' but wouldn't order the item again."

"Oh," I uttered, feeling the disappointment for my presumptuous interruption.

"What I do is look at plates of the specials as they're being brought back into the kitchen. We give them, I confess, a larger portion than we would normally. But by seeing how much they ate of the course in question I can determine how much they enjoyed it."

The educational supervisor or administrator employs a similar technique. He listens to children leaving a classroom to hear their conversations. If they are excited by a lesson they tend to continue talking about it after leaving the class. Learning depends on interest, which does not subside instantaneously at a session-ending bell. It gurgles a bit before sinking beneath the surface. One conversation and one class meeting is insufficient for a serious rating of a lesson, but the accumulation of evidence from this source added to other observations becomes a good indicator. The applicant was correct. You don't have to know the subject to evaluate general effort and performance. The parent doesn't have to know the subject either to know if her child is making good progress. Therefore, whenever a parent detects a weakness in one or more subjects, she should utilize the recommendations for improving general learning capability delineated in the chapters cited.

Parent–Child, Parent–School Communication

As covered earlier, for effective communication to take place, listening skills must be developed. There is also another explanation for communication failure, which involves the different interpretations attending parties may make of words and phrases. Spoken language, which helps separate humans from all other species, extraordinarily brilliant as it is, is not perfect. Sometimes words cannot be translated with full meaning from language to language. A nuance may be lost. Differences of usage by people supposedly speaking the same tongue may also lead to misinterpretation and confusion.

A state official was visiting a private school for a preevaluative meeting. He was to be followed at a later date by a team. The school director, sitting at lunch with the official and me, a school consultant, was trying to set the stage for a favorable impression. The school actually, in my view, was as good as schools get in terms of programs, electromechanical aids of all kinds, books, and general supplies. The administrators, supervisors, and specialists not only had first rate credentials, which would please a government official, but were unusually dedicated and competent, which pleased me. The ratio of staff to pupil was outstanding, and the school routinely performed educational, psychological, and medical examinations.

The director found an opening in the conversation to discuss the strongest point of all, the teachers. Not only was every teacher certified precisely in the area she taught, but even the aides, who were plentiful, were all college graduates. In addition, there were in-house, fully qualified substitute teachers, who were not only available as needed and familiar with the children and curriculum of the teacher they might have to replace, but provided, when the regular teachers were present, individual instruction to children who could profit from it. The director should have let the school speak for itself but couldn't resist an opportunity to praise her staff.

"My teachers?" she asked of a question. She smiled and confidently stressed "My teachers are bad," using a deliberately broad 'a.' In her view "bad" in this context meant just the opposite of the traditional meaning of the word. Bad, as she used it, she thought, meant not just good but exceedingly good. Ba-a-a-d was praise.

The startled official interpreted the word by its classic usage. Bad means what it always means: poor, unacceptable. Such an evaluation of her staff didn't fit with the accolades he had heard from visitors and parents. It didn't fit with the director's manner, which indicated pride. Something wasn't right but he wasn't yet sure what that might be. Was she setting him up for a surprise or confession to a weakness she knew he would perceive? He diplomatically avoided responding orally, but his face revealed caution.

Since I was sitting on the sidelines, I could ascertain both sides of the communication; I quickly explained how she was using the word "bad" and how he was interpreting it. The simple statement put them both on the same track, but had the misunderstanding not been clarified, there could have been long-term unfavorable consequences.

If two educators could miscommunicate, so could you as a parent with a school official or with your child. If you are speaking with a teacher and you are not clear about a statement or a word, leave your pride elsewhere and ask questions.

A Check of Understanding

Now, let's back up for a moment to get a full picture of your adolescent's situation. You are certain that you understand what your child's teachers, counselors, or other school personnel are saying about him. You are sure that you know what he says about himself. You also know that what he says may not be what he really thinks or feels and may actually reveal how much he doesn't know about himself.

You are confident that your offspring is an underachiever. You have determined this yourself, irrespective of what others may have ascertained. You have utilized the material suggested earlier and have adapted it to fit your child and yourself.

He is not just underachieving in a particular subject. He is underachieving across the board with the possible exception of areas of high interest. You have carefully examined the record.

He is not suffering the effects of a neurological disturbance, nor does he have a debilitating sensory deficit. You have professional confirmation of this view.

He is not likely to be learning disabled according to the accepted definitions. He is capable of learning subjects presented by the school at his grade level. He doesn't fail; he just doesn't do as well as he should. You are satisfied that he performs substantially below his innate capacity (making you dissatisfied).

Working at Home

"Is he working?" the father asked his wife. She had just descended the stairs into the living room, carrying a newspaper to be discarded.

"I don't know," she responded plaintively. "I passed his room a couple of times and glanced in. He's sitting there, at his desk, but doesn't seem to be writing or reading. Just sitting."

"He's been there for two hours; maybe he's finished," the man pointed out.

"Yes, but maybe he doesn't want to come down. He knows you want him to clean the garage. Maybe he's just stalling."

"You're probably right. He's lazy all right. Otherwise, with his ability he'd do a lot better in school. I'm going to look in on him," said the husband rising from the sofa.

"Don't start anything with him," advised the woman. "We don't need another argument like last Saturday."

"I know. I know. I'll just ask if he needs help and if he says 'No' I'll leave."

"Suppose he says 'Yes,' what'll you do? How's your algebra?"

"I was good at algebra," the man protested.

"The operant word is 'was.' What can you do now?"

"Not much, I guess," he grudgingly acknowledged. "But if he needs help, we'll find him a math tutor."

"What about his other subjects? A tutor for each one?"

"Maybe that learning center is what he needs. They cover all subjects."

"What about the costs?"

"If we didn't have to have a new car right now, I'd say it was worth it. I . . ." He paused, then smiled at his wife.

"I know, the operant word is 'If,' " he said, as he headed for his son's room.

"Math problems?" Jeff's father asked standing at the door.

"No. Actually it's a history assignment giving me fits."

"History? That doesn't sound too complex," said the father with growing confidence. "Maybe I can help. What do you have to do?"

"It's the Civil War. I've got to give a report."

"All right," said the father taking command. "I see you have your textbook handy and the encyclopedia is right there. It'll have plenty on the Civil War. Those books may be a little old but I'm sure the facts on that war are still the same." Jeff's father smiled, pleased with his observation.

"Won't help," announced the glum Jeff.

"Why not?" his father shot back. "The facts haven't changed."

"That's not the assignment. The facts, so called, are all spelled out. My report is on how the South could have avoided the conflict, stayed in the Union, and still maintained their voting strength in the Senate."

The man stared at his son, quickly understanding that he didn't understand.

"Well, I'm sure you can handle it," he said, feigning confidence. "I just came to tell you to stick with the schoolwork and that I'm going to clean the garage myself," he fibbed.

"Okay, Dad. Thanks."

Jeff glanced at the clock. He had agreed to a fixed time for homework. Only fifteen minutes to go, he noted, and he'd get his parents off his back. He was unconcerned about the unfinished assignment.

Jeff's parents illustrate many thousands who do not know how to provide viable assistance. The parents, in this case, are lamenting over their financial inability to provide tutors or a learning center. Jeff doesn't need either. He doesn't need to overcome laziness. His needs are similar to Mary's.

Mary, complaining to her favorite teacher, noted that her parents expect too much of her. She applied herself to her work as well as she could. In fact, she realized, she spent many more hours on homework than her friends.

"It's mostly my Mom. My father agrees with her but he doesn't bug me too much. Mom is after me all the time. 'You can do better. You can do better.' It's such a pain."

"Can you do better?" asked the teacher, hoping that Mary would consider another approach.

"Sure. Everybody can do a little better, right? But I can't do what my Mom expects."

"What does she expect?"

"Higher grades. Look, I pass every single subject. I never get anything less than a C and sometimes I get a B, like in your class. I'm average and maybe even better than average. Isn't that good enough?" Mary paused to formulate another thought.

"You know, parents always think their kids are smarter than they really are, right?"

"Sometimes," said the teacher, avoiding the generalization. "In this case, Mary, they are right. Your grades are substantially below your ability. They should be well above average, at least."

Mary enjoyed the warm internal glow resulting from the flattery as she listened to her teacher's comments. She really had some brains, she told herself. Parents exaggerate but teachers are with it. They have all that training. College and stuff. And they read a lot. Parents just want, but teachers know.

"Do you really think I should get higher grades?" Mary asked, seeking one last compliment.

Her teacher sensed Mary's new interest in higher performance. "Mary, intelligence doesn't mean you get a free ride. You have to work and work hard. If you do, you'll become one of the better students in your class."

Mary's teacher wasn't quite right on the last point. Working harder than before would produce only minimal improvement. Mary, as Jeff, faced a deficit neither she, nor her teacher, nor her parents recognized.

An Unrecognized Educational Malady

Mary and Jeff and Bill, mentioned earlier, are illustrative of a minority, but still numerous, group of underachievers who lack efficient task attack skills. A weakness of this sort tends to go unrecognized for a variety of reasons. The ability to confront a challenge in some meaningful and efficient way is necessary for most people during their lives. Every normal person can resolve some problems some of the time, which only shrouds the seriousness and extent of the disability. The operational deficit exists not only in school but also in the work world.

A very trite but well-founded adage advises bosses with a rush job to give it to their busiest employees. These busy people have learned how to reorder their priorities so that the most important items that are due the earliest are done first. That is only their first step. They know, or quickly determine, how to complete the task while economizing time. Without formalizing a detailed procedure, they draw up a mental plan to accomplish the task. Then, unlike many of their colleagues, they get started without unnecessary delay. If they're interrupted by someone who has an even greater priority, they are able to return to the original task in the shortest possible time without undue stress.

Jayne, working in a state department of education, although conscientious and hardworking, was not one of these busy people. On this particular day she was confronted with a problem that always caused her stress. She had to make a decision by herself without a precedent to serve as a guideline and without others to make meaningful suggestions.

"Jayne, this letter came in last week from the superintendent of this small school district," said her supervisor. "He's right in directing his query to us about meeting the minimum number of days requested for the school year. It is a state matter, you know. If a district falls below the required calendar, they're apt to lose some state funds.

"Anyhow, look at these activities he wants to count as school days. Harris, Carol, and I discussed it and decided that these substitute activities shouldn't count. So answer him and give him some explanation."

"But George, I can't make that decision. I . . ."

"You're not making the decision. We've already made it . . . and Jayne, sign your own name."

Jayne, for the next three hours, showed the superintendent's letter to all her available colleagues, who offered no comments. She made phone calls trying to elicit views from friends who were not in their offices. She discussed it with her secretary and a visitor to her bureau. She received no help. A review of the regulations and a search of the files revealed no clear path to follow. She had to answer the letter on her own.

As lunchtime approached, she called her secretary to take dictation. No other work had been done all morning as she fretted over this "unreasonable" assignment.

"Okay. I've decided what I'm going to do. Tell the superintendent this. His request for special credit days is denied pending a thorough review of all facets of the consequences of an approval of the request. Should he seek further clarification, he should address his questions directly to the bureau director. Then give him the usual 'if we can be of any help in the future' and so on. Got it? Put it into the right words," she instructed her secretary. "I'll sign it after lunch."

Why They Don't Have Task Attack Skills

Unjustified Assumptions. The high school teacher assumes that task attack skills have been taught and mastered at some acceptable level during the elementary grades. The employer assumes high school graduates and certainly college graduates know how to complete an assignment. Too often, the assumptions and reality differ markedly.

Misleading Performance. Students at all levels of education may get through with only minimal task attack skills. Just as with intelligence, everyone has some. Every normal person has the ability to perform at some level, but when that level is substantially below their real capability, the student earns C's instead of A's.

Disguised Ability. High-level people in industry, commerce, and government find that many job applicants who have outstanding credentials, high written test scores, and favorable ratings in interviews cannot perform adequately on the job. Many people can give quick and satisfactory answers to hypothetical questions presented in both written and oral examinations. Their native ability stands them in good stead. However, confronted by real problems and deadlines, underachievers in the workplace become detriments to the organization. Their opportunities for promotion or even to retain their positions are minimal.

Premature Training Programs. In school and in vocational settings, thoughtful administrators provide specialized curricula in the context of formal instruction, coaching, and manuals to help the learner master a new position. If the novice on a job lacks the fundamental skills for learning and utilizing complex material, the training may not prepare him to evaluate the job at the expected level of competence.

Symptoms Mask the Cause. A learner may avoid certain subjects in which he has had previous negative experiences, or he may resist being forced into situations where he doubts the possibility of success. If forced into such situations, he may react emotionally or with unruly acts. The parent and the professional may then ascribe his failure to perform satisfactorily to his unacceptable behavior—the symptom, rather than the cause, which is really a lack of a basic skill.

It Doesn't Exist. Efficient use of task attack skills does not generally exist as a subject, such as biology or English literature. Many thoughtful teachers do review such techniques as they present content material in their specialities. However, underachievers are usually scattered within the school system, cause few problems, and are not typically placed in a separate classification such as the retarded or the gifted. The problem is compounded further since only some underachievers suffer from the effects of this weakness. Most are underachievers for quite different reasons.

Parental Role

You probably are not aware of your child's task attack skill level, and there are surely other problems that are contributing to his unsatisfactory performance, which may be identified and remediated. However, a weakness in this particular area will constrain his scholarship now and later. Any improvement in attack skills will affect his performance favorably. The worst that can happen is that he'll quickly demonstrate proficiency in this area. More likely, even if he possesses a good grip on learning skills, a review of the basics will only serve to hone them to an even sharper level.

Let's return to our two C students who have an A or at least a B+ ability. Jeff is overwhelmed by some assignments, for example his history report. He is presented with a mass of material on a subject and has no idea how to crystallize this huge blob into workable elements. The feeling will be familiar to many readers. You are faced with multiple tasks requiring your immediate attention without receiving specific directions from an authority telling you what you must do first, second, and so on. Do it, you're instructed. Do it your way, but do it. That's what happened to Jayne, the bureaucrat.

But I don't have a way, you would like to protest. What you really want is a way out of the situation. Let someone else do it. But it's your assignment, or your job, or your problem. Why me? you groan. Why do I have to do it?

"Just do one piece at a time," you're told. Which piece? The challenge may be a daunting one. If it was preceded by similar experiences, which are still unresolved, and you know that there will be more to come in the future, you may fall into a funk. Worse, you may divorce yourself from reality, hide from the problem, and do nothing. If the state of your adjustment is negative enough, you may even become psychologically depressed. Now you have another problem.

Neither Jeff nor Mary are near a state of depression, and both make attempts to do some of the work. With effort and time, most of it unproductive, they manage to get something done. They avoid failure by working hard at accomplishing little. Jeff spent two hours and ten minutes on the history assignment without having completed anything of consequence. Jayne, who is an adult version of Mary, spent half a day deciding how to respond to a routine letter. Her superior, when he needed someone to do an important chore, didn't select her. He knew better. He gave her what he thought was an ordinary assignment. The decision not to approve the request had already been made.

Jeff faced a sizable challenge. If his assignment had not required decision making or could be gleaned simply from reading text material, he could have handled it well. He did well in familiar assignments, which is what kept him from drowning scholastically.

Mary had difficulty deciding on how to do a problem. She would like to have started with the answer in mind, but that wasn't always possible. When she did get moving, she didn't always know where she was going or when she arrived there. She rarely had a clear picture of her goal in learning.

Jayne created many of her own problems. She managed to get through school with satisfactory grades but spent more time on her studies than the rest of her classmates. Despite her superior intelligence, she earned only run-of-the-mill grades. She has advanced from being an underachieving student to being an underachieving adult. She has not learned to collect all of the available facts, place them into some logical order, and make an educated decision based on the information before her. She prefers someone else to decide, which is not always possible. Without decision-making practice, she has little confidence in her own judgment. Even after deciding, once the decision is irreversible, she wonders if she has done the right thing for a prolonged period of time.

Jayne adjusts to her shortcoming by telling everyone she is exceptionally flexible, by postponing decisions whenever and as long as possible, and by changing her mind whenever she can. For instance, she shops only in stores with a liberal return policy.

Jeff, Mary, and Jayne all lack well-developed, task organizational procedures. Jayne has adjusted to this weakness both in school and on the job by working longer hours than necessary. In the example given, Jayne frittered away most of the morning on a nonchallenging assignment. As a consequence, other work was not completed, but she finished these other tasks at home.

Had Jayne learned a more sophisticated approach to tasks while still in school, while expending the same effort, she would have been an overachiever. Jeff and Mary, however, were not willing to make the additional effort. Not understanding the cause of their problems, they assumed their native abilities were overrated by their parents.

All parents, especially those of underachieving children, should focus on helping their children learn how to learn. The following is a plan of action suitable for application by the parent of the adolescent.

Parent-Directed Attack Skills

The student, and later the adult in the workplace, both need a starting point for confronting any task. The parent is concerned with scholarship at this stage of her teenager's life. Therefore, the techniques described are directed toward this end. However, they are highly transferrable. Problem solving is a facet of living at every age. These methods will soon become part of the automatic response mechanism of the subject, similar to playing a game of mental skill, such as chess. The player has to think about the situation confronting him but doesn't have to review all of the possible strategies. His supercomputer subconscious dismisses a host of possible moves and narrows his choices down to just a few for his conscious mind to select.

Initially, the subconscious is not involved. The parent, for a time, must point to the appropriate step to keep the learner on track. The minds of the two students described earlier frequently wander about without actually getting started in a meaningful way. To ensure that the learner, or worker, gets started on the right track, first a plan of action should be developed. Initially, the plan should be in writing and designed for the individual in question. The parent of an elementary school child can sit next to the learner and personally direct the study operation. However, the adolescent is not usually so disposed. He may reject being treated as a child. The parent would be accused of "interfering."

"Don't tell me what to do. I know what to do. What do you know about this subject?"

You will not get away with telling him you can evaluate his learning without knowing the language. You need not explain that you're only trying to help with the broad underpinnings of learning techniques, not the discipline itself. Instead, you can prepare directions that he may use, tailored to him as you and you alone understand him, based on the examples provided below.

You want to get that learning machine rolling. You need a powerful low gear. Later, the learner can shift into high and complete the task. These items are designed to provide the student with the initial steps that will help him make sense out of a project and formulate a plan to complete the assignment. In the beginning, he will consider each item separately. Later, after some practice, he'll jump right in and omit those items not necessary in the specific effort.

Step One: Getting Started

The reluctance to *start* an assignment is a major obstacle. The individual is doing something much more interesting at the moment. If he isn't, he can quickly find something. This obstacle is faced by everyone on a very frequent basis. People overcome their resistance to start a chore by recognizing an obligation or the possibility of a reward for a completed task. The parent can arrange a discussion on obligations at the roundtable, where all the participants can relate their gripes and experiences.

The parent should use two kinds of rewards as incentives. One is the satisfaction of learning and completing an assignment. The other is an overt reward: high test scores, good grades, and a parental payoff such as the cancellation of a prior "grounding," tickets to a ball game, or an extension of the usual curfew hour.

The underachiever, however, may be disinclined to start because of another reason. He has too many experiences of getting lost in the quagmire of homework. Once he has formulated a working plan that will enable him to attack his challenge both efficiently and effectively, however, the foot-dragging will diminish.

Each individual must design a personal program, one that works for him. Each time he employs his own strategies, his skill sharpens. Even the underachiever will notice that the task becomes less difficult with practice. In or out of school, challenges are less forbidding if the individual is prepared. A framework for developing the learner's techniques follows.

Step Two: Implementation

1. Decide what to do. Read the entire assignment carefully. Summarize it mentally, or if it is too long, in writing. If it is a chapter in a book, skim over the chapter.
2. Determine what information is required to complete the task. If the assignment is complex, make a list of data needed to do the job.
3. Examine the material in the text and the notes. Is the information required available? If not, where may it be acquired? Collect the facts needed before starting.
4. Ascertain the main theme of the assignment. What is to be learned? What are the most important elements? What

bits of information could be omitted without disturbing the continuity and clarity of the answer? For instance, the essence of the assignment could be:

(a) The economic depression of the 1930s could have been the inevitable consequence of the overheated expansion of the twenties.
(b) The mysterious "black holes" in space might lend themselves to startling new astronomical theories.
(c) The field of psychology could still learn much from Shakespeare's understanding of human motivation.

5. Arrange the important items in some sequence that seems logical. What would make a good beginning? What order should the facts in the middle be in? What is the best conclusion? Read over the sequence. Does it flow? Are there omissions? Rearrange and fill in the material if necessary.
6. Ask questions about the assignment as a final check to the arrangement. What is to be learned? Why was the assignment given? What was studied before that relates to this current material?
7. Examine the length of the assignment. Should it be separated into segments for easier handling? Can the entire assignment be completed at one sitting or should part of it be scheduled for another time?
8. Consider the strategy to be employed to complete the assignment. Did the teacher suggest an approach? Does the assignment resemble homework of the past? Is there a successful format from earlier homework that might be applicable to this one? What strategies might be employed to complete the work accurately? What is the best option of those available?
9. Before beginning the actual work, recheck. Is the assignment clear? Are the objectives apparent? Are the materials and facts available? Is a reasonable estimate of time required for completion now determined? When, precisely, will the task be completed?

10. *Start now.* Don't test the pool water with your toes. Dive right in.

Step Three: Evaluation

1. Are the objectives reached? Are the answers clear? Will the teacher know what was done?
2. Is each segment of the assignment understandable? Can each component be explained? Are there any gaps that should have been filled?
3. What was learned? Was anything learned that wasn't originally planned? How may this knowledge be used?
4. Is the written presentation of the work neat, clear, and ready for submission?
5. What was learned about systems and strategies to do this assignment? How may these be utilized next time?

Step Four: Reinforcement

The learner should use the task attack skills that work for him as an individual. The parent should see, however, that there is a coherent plan. Many underachievers dab at the fringes of the work instead of determining the essence of the assignment before starting. A discouraging but frequent outcry can be heard from a student after an hour of labor: "I didn't know I had to do that!"

The more the learner works on the preparation to do the assignment, the shorter and easier the assignment becomes. The measures suggested above, after a few weeks of use, become internalized, and the learner employs them without conscious thought. The techniques developed to do homework are useful in taking subjective tests, just as the listening techniques used in the roundtable are utilized effectively in the classroom.

Task attack skills are nothing more than systematizing methods of learning and focusing on the task at hand. The ease with which these procedures are mastered and the favorable results that follow build confidence in the underachiever.

Reading Assignments

As with extensive assignments, a parental-offered strategy for reading assignments is designed to simplify the work as much as possible. You want the learner to grasp the most important aspects of the topic, but in high school, he need not learn a myriad of details. He will learn some since many of the details will cling to the main points. Details of some subjects are without limit. No teacher would expect her adolescent students to remember every battle of the Civil War, even if she considered battles to be important, but a science teacher may expect her students to identify every planet in our solar system since there are only nine. The history teacher will probably be more interested in having the students learn about the causes of the Civil War and their aftereffects. The science teacher will probably focus on the four forces identified in the universe and not on the names given to the various moons.

The parent should ask her teenager to tell her about the areas where the teacher places an emphasis. By merely reviewing the teacher's position, the student will learn which items are the important ones. The student will be helping himself without much of a conscious realization that he is reviewing class instruction. The parent, of course, must truly be listening.

The emphasis on highlights applies to reading the subject matter from a textbook. Parental involvement and questions should focus on the main items in the content of the reading material. Again, the learner should not get lost in extraneous detail and tangential material. The underachiever will frequently read the chapter assigned, close the book, and go on to something more interesting. He's read it, he's done what he's supposed to do, now let him alone.

"Did you do your homework?"

"Yeah, I finished it."

"What did you have to do?"

"Read chapters four, five, and six."

"And you did?"

"Yeah."

"All of it."

"Yeah."

"All right."

No. It's not all right if the learner is an underachiever. The parent has to ask some questions to determine if the assignment has been completed adequately. The parent need not be familiar with the subject matter if she follows some rules that consist of looking at and listening to the student. If he has read the material *with comprehension,* he will be able to answer your general questions with minimal hesitation, with a degree of certitude, and with clarity. If he falls back on "Mom, you wouldn't understand!" make *him* understand that this type of response is unacceptable. If he claims he knows the material but can't explain it, he doesn't know the material well enough.

The thought processes involved in answering your questions will help him organize the content of the material he has studied and reinforce it so that he will retain it better. If he hasn't really mastered it, he'll know you know. He must return to his assignment and review it again.

The questions listed below may be adapted to almost all kinds of reading material. The exact wording is unimportant. You want *him* to think and explain.

- What did you read?
- What else was in it?
- Explain the material as if you were telling a classmate about it.
- How does it fit with earlier studies?
- Should something have been covered that wasn't?
- What does all of this mean?
- How can you use this information?

The fundamentals of learning apply, in some fashion, to all subjects. By displaying an active interest in your child's work, you are taking two vital steps. You are helping him realize that a cursory approach to an assignment may get him by, but to do his best he must truly apply himself. In addition, as the new understanding of teenagers provided earlier reveals, he wants you, despite his protests, to be interested in his world. Your concern will impress him and overshadow your use of your authority, which is rapidly diminishing. Knowing that you care enough to take the time to help him with schoolwork will have a lasting effect, while a "Because I say so" approach may be useful only for the short term. "Do your homework" is all right for most students. But where the underachiever is concerned, parents must be more active.

You may think you're too busy to devote time to this program. That's not true. The actual review time as indicated for a high school assignment takes less than ten minutes. As the student grasps the significance of your questions, he will learn to read more carefully the first time and prepare answers for the questions he knows are coming. This reduces the review time and, more importantly, makes him a better learner.

All task attack skills, no matter how laboriously explained, may be reduced to a few essentials. What is to be learned? What is the best strategy to employ? Are the essential elements and materials readily available, and, if not, where can they be obtained? What is a reasonable time effort? What checks of progress may be used? How will the final result appear? How may the completed task be evaluated?

By working with your adolescent to review his learning system,

- You are showing an interest in him personally, which helps satisfy his need for parental love and strengthens the bond between you. You are becoming an ally instead of a task master.
- You are formally offering systems that he will need throughout life, strengthening the adequate structures and identifying weak areas that can be improved. These changes will elevate his confidence level.
- You are making him aware of the underlying methodology

for learning that is so vital in school, at work, and in the social world.

Wrap-Up

One broken rung on the learning ladder could cause a student to stumble and fall. Since the parent may not know precisely where the weak rung is, she should review the whole learning process. The most difficult challenge for many parents is to realize how really easy learning can become.

Every component of a learning technique is so obvious that adults might refrain from mentioning it. They, as parents, assume that the student knows them already. But if the learner omits one essential step or doesn't, on review, identify an error, his whole effort may become time consuming and frustrating. Experience also shows that the learner may repeat similar mistakes of omission or commission in later assignments. All of the pieces must be assembled properly for the successful completion of each task.

The parent should review the questions provided for the learner to use and have him apply them to each assignment.

"Oh, Mom. Come on. I know that."

Of course he does. It's just too much trouble to employ a checklist, but it's an effective way to reduce wasted effort and master a subject.

Learning skills vary according to individuals, and each student must use whatever works best for him. The underachiever should apply the guiding questions enumerated earlier to each assignment. With use, two changes will take place. First, they'll become an integral part of his learning mechanism. He won't have to ask each question or supply an answer every time. As with operating an automobile, he'll just use the system without conscious self-direction. Second, again without trying, he will modify the questions to fit his own unique mental structures. This, too, will become automatic. In the beginning, however, the parent should review the suggestions, step by step, until the student demonstrates a sufficient mastery.

A difficulty that the parent must overcome to be successful is the reluctance to pose as a "teacher." It's not a parent's job to teach subject matter or subject skills. Instead, the parent should suggest a learning technique—a methodology that will be applicable to all disciplines. If the student follows some reasonable organizational pattern, he will rarely face insurmountable problems.

The student may suggest that he knows all of this, or that he has his own favorite shortcut. Insist that he still use the techniques as outlined and question him on them. Shortcuts are for the A student.

An essential ingredient called "interest" may be developed over time by having the student participate in the family roundtable. He will begin to see interrelationships between and among seemingly disparate fields and their value in the "real" world. Involving him, listening to him, and encouraging him will help bring about a feeling of success, which will start a snowball effect.

The operations of the mind are still enigmatic, but there is no mystery about learning systems. Interest, organization, developing confidence, and repeated experiences with success, in combination, will yield the desired results.

15

Reacting to Setbacks

"Ready?"

"I sure am," replied Glen to his father's query.

"I'll bet you didn't sleep too well last night. It's natural, you know, to be nervous. First game of the season and all that."

"I slept fine, Dad. I did okay in practice. I'll do fine today. Hey. What can happen to me?"

Glen stopped to reflect on his own question. What could happen? He's the pitcher. He'll just go up there and throw his fastball right past those batters. He can do it, too. Didn't the coach choose him over Snuffy for the opening day game? And Snuffy is good, too.

"How's your arm feel?"

"Great, Dad." He swung his right arm 360 degrees, as if it were a propeller. He then did the same for his left one, as if to avoid jealousy.

"Everything's fine. I'm ready. Let's go."

His parents grabbed some sweaters, although the forecast called for seventy-plus temperatures. Chub, his kid brother, took along his own glove, but the eleven-year-old wasn't on the team. It was for teenagers only.

In just half an hour, Glen and his family were at the baseball field. The stands were packed, mostly with parents. The visitors were batting first and Glen was underhanding the ball to his catcher.

"Okay Glen, let 'er fly," came the voice from behind the mask. Glen did. Then again. Then once more. The spheroid had no guidance system but found its target on a corner of home plate each time.

Gary, the catcher, stood smiling as if the game were over. Victory was certain. No one told the visitors.

"Play ball!" yelled the umpire, and the disaster began.

Strike one. Strike two on the lead-off batter. Throw another fastball said the spider to the fly. Glen did, and the batter was on first after he stroked the ball between the shortstop and the second-base bag.

The next hitter for the visitors was more obliging. He hit a line drive right at the first baseman, who was crouched three feet from the bag. The runner was off toward second. The fielder merely had to catch the ball and step on the base for a double play. Two outs. He stepped on the base but without the ball, which now was rolling down the line to the right-field wall.

Glen, upset by the events, walked the next batter on four straight pitches. Bases loaded. Gary and the manager hustled out to the mound to settle their pitcher down.

The cleanup batter was next. "This guy is Casey at the bat," noted the manager. Remember our discussion before the game? He's a sucker for a high fastball. He'll reach every time. Go get him, kid. Give him the smoke."

Glen told himself repeatedly: High heat. High heat. Gary signaled with two fingers and then one. High fastball. Glen threw. Perfect. High and fast. The batter swung and the ball sailed into left field, high and fast. The left fielder heard it crack into the fence before he could reach it. Three runs home. Runner on second. Nobody out.

Gary could see the manager again entering the playing field; this time his eyes avoided the pitcher. The manager gave the signal

Glen never thought he would see—relief pitcher, come in. Glen was through. Snuffy was coming in to replace him.

Glen's brother was right but he didn't want to hear it anymore. All the way home, he repeated the observation. "It should have been a double play. If that first baseman, what's his name, had caught that ball, Glen would have shut them out. The whole game. Shut them out."

"There will be another day," Glen's mother observed.

Glen's family was on his side, but somehow that didn't seem to help. He was going to be the star, the pitcher everyone in the league would fear. What happened? He didn't get anyone out. He let in three quick runs. He looked good in training but couldn't cut it when the games counted. Maybe if those guys were great hitters, it wouldn't be as bad. But then Snuffy went in and pitched out of the inning. No further damage. Snuffy went the rest of the game giving up only two additional runs. The visitors finally won five to four. Glen was the losing pitcher on the record book. Some star, he thought.

At dinner that evening Glen's father reviewed every pitch Glen had thrown. They discussed each batter Glen had faced and what was known about his hitting ability, his weaknesses, and his strengths. While Glen felt somewhat unhappy about his poor performance, his father was seriously perturbed. The parent had allowed himself to engage in some bragging at work and had made the error of predicting how well his son would shine in the opening-day game.

One of Glen's father's co-workers had noted that the prediction was unrealistic. "Look, one game. Anything can happen in one game. The best pitchers in baseball get shelled sometimes."

The father, however, was caught up in his own prophesies and couldn't back off. Now he had to face his colleagues on Monday without an excuse for Glen's performance. But hold on. Maybe it wasn't Glen's fault. He replayed each event in his mind.

The whole thing would have been different if the first baseman had caught the ball and made the double play as he should have. Glen's brother was right on target pointing that out. But look. There's more. The manager insisted on giving the cleanup batter a high fastball. That's exactly what Glen did. He followed orders explicitly. The pitch was exactly what the manager asked for and the batter hit it. Was that Glen's fault?

Then what does the manager do? He yanks Glen from the game. The kid only faced four batters. He would have settled down. Maybe he would have shut out the visitors the rest of the way and Glen's team would have won. Sure. Glen did what he was told to do and got the blame when things went wrong. Well, Glen's father thought, feeling better now, I'll explain all this to the guys at work. In the meantime he felt compelled to assuage Glen's feelings.

"Hey Glen. You didn't do so badly. It was bad fielding and poor coaching that cost us that game."

Dealing with Setbacks

One of the major causes of underachievement in life is a failure to bounce back adequately after a disappointment. Children learn early that certain responses will bring them comfort after an event that was not to their liking. All aspects of living are involved in a decision-making process, but the one a child learns to utilize in his educational effort may affect virtually everything else. The young child tries for a good grade, studies for a test, earns a disappointing mark, and is thoroughly confused. The parent intervenes on the child's behalf with encouragement and suggestions on doing better the next time. If the parent provides the appropriate measures on a consistent basis, the child, with deep faith in the parent's judgmental abilities, will go on to overcome the earlier disappointment. A thorn is removed from the emotional development of the child, and both cognition and affectivity are developing optimally.

The adolescent faces somewhat different circumstances when

confronted with a disappointment. The teenager doesn't have quite the same faith in the parent's recommendations and discounts their encouragement as just something all parents do. The adolescent, by nature of his mental growth stage, is now looking inward and analyzing himself.

Where did I go wrong?
Was I adequately prepared?
Am I good enough to meet this challenge?
Were the circumstances against me or did I just fail?

The last item may be a realistic evaluation leading to a change in preparation or practice and a new effort. Or, unfortunately, it may lead to a serious miscalculation with severe ramifications for the future. The case of Glen and his father illustrates the possibility.

An everyday event of no substantial consequence in a person's life may be inflated to affect, adversely, that person's attitude to a host of happenings that may follow. Glen's father, in this case, found the explanation that humans have used for eons to excuse failure and to justify an action not otherwise acceptable. The father found an excuse in the form of blaming other people. The first baseman didn't catch the ball, the manager called for the wrong pitch, and Glen was removed from the game prematurely. Glen failed but someone else caused the failure.

Glen initially didn't consider blaming others for his poor performance, even when his brother reminded him of the faulty fielding behind him. But when his father exculpated him from poor pitching and pointed elsewhere, the thought was planted in Glen's mind. So now another line may be added to the introspection.

Others share the responsibility for my failure or, even, others *caused* my failure.

The parent should help a teenager understand incidents involving educational and social disappointments, but that intervention must be thought out very carefully. Some basic approaches should dictate the form of the assistance provided by the parent.

Avoid Reinforcing Negatives. The game of life is no more perfect than the game of baseball. Errors of omission, commission, and judgment will occur. Most people claim that they have experienced more than their share of unfavorable circumstances. Each youth should understand that fate has not chosen just him for undesirable happenstances. Everyone faces them. One of the most commonly utilized expressions is "With my luck . . ." Statistically and logically, everyone has the same chance at good or bad luck if the conditions are equal.

Accept the Responsibility for the Results. Admitting that the adolescent's weakness or lack of effort was the reason for the failure is part of the mending process. Certainly others may have been involved in some activities and some may have offered poor advice or neglected to fulfill their obligations. But these are facts to build on. By analyzing his own performance, the teenager may discover that he failed because he relied on others to do his job. He can see for future reference what type of preparation he requires to overcome his particular weaknesses and how to take better advantage of his individual assets. He must, through parental action, come to understand that most failures are not final verdicts but learning experiences. If the learner, himself, understands his own past experiences, then, as with history, he will not be condemned to repeat his mistakes.

Overcome the Fear of Failing While It Is Still Incubating. Once an adolescent is stunned by rejection, dashed hopes, underperformance, and wrong choices in a particular type of effort, he may develop an uncalled-for aversion to such an effort. In school, this could be a particular subject that is either new—algebra, for instance—or one in which he had high expectations followed by disappointment. The subject may become anathema to him and cause for avoidance from there on. A distinction must be made between those subjects or activities that a person cannot do well because of an innate weakness and those that have developed from a negative association due to past underperformance. A fear of failing in a given area may become a great inhibitor and obstacle to progress.

The traditional adage that if you fall off a horse you must get back on very soon is applicable. Avoid allowing the negative experience to grow into a near or complete phobia.

"Glen, get back in there and pitch. Throw that high fastball right past the batter."

Establish Realistic Expectations. There is no one accepted number of times any person should try to overcome a particular obstacle. Striving is a paramount ingredient in most successes. A failure may be followed by a failure without compounding a defeatist attitude. The student usually turns things around gradually. The process becomes more important than each individual result. The key in any effort is "improvement." The underachiever is not likely to turn a C into an A on the next examination, although this is not unheard of. More likely, the C will climb the ladder, rung by rung, perhaps skipping a step here and there. Although each student and each parent would love to see the low grades turn into the highest immediately, the steady climb to the top will have a lasting and transferable effect.

Use Past Experience to Overcome Obstacles. Success, of course, will pave the way for continued success. After following the advice offered earlier, you have assessed your child based not only on numbers but on his behavior under various conditions over the years. You know your underachiever has done some things very well or, simply, that he has been successful at times. Now is the time to bring one dramatic success into focus even if it is unrelated to the current activity. Learning is transferable, and the adolescent will be able to draw an inference from a past successful experience; that is, with some extra effort he can apply similar skills to the current challenge. The emotional tie-in with that past effort that bore fruit will help him organize and utilize appropriate skills to attack the new problem. Remember: emotion is tied directly to cognition. Past successful experiences, brought to the fore, will help to make his attitude more positive.

Parental Understandings

Patricia Cummings was an outstanding history student for reasons that her parents failed to comprehend. The psychologist examining her also missed the point. Patricia did very well in some school subjects, while she just managed to get by in others. Examples of her extremes were history and mathematics.

Anyone with an I.Q. of 128 should breeze through high school mathematics, the psychologist felt. Obviously, it's not a lack of capability but some other obstructing problem. The history is easily explained, he argued. History is a matter of memorizing events, maybe dates, some names, and material that the teacher presents to complement the material in the textbook. Pat, with her intelligence, has no trouble regurgitating the facts she studies in their proper place. Thus, she receives high grades. Math is something else. Math is little memorization but the application of cognitive skill in applying logic to abstract situations.

"The manipulation of symbols is not for everyone," he reported to Mrs. Cummings. "Some people, very intelligent people, just can't do well beyond basic arithmetic. These same people may excel in other subjects. Pat fits this group. Math low, history high."

Pat's mother sat still, thinking about his comments. The psychologist provided an afterthought.

"Girls, you know. Math. The physical sciences. Not their forte."

Armed with this misinformation, Pat's mother returned home to discuss the meeting with her husband.

"He says that with more effort Pat could do a little better, but she's never going to do well in areas such as geometry and algebra. He says it's not uncommon for girls to have trouble in mathematics."

"She did well her first eight years in school. Why the change?" asked the father.

"He answered that. He says in elementary school girls may keep up but start to lose out when math gets complex. They usually don't do well in some other subjects, too. Chemistry. Physics."

"But she does so well in other subjects. History, for instance," the father noted.

"That's just memorization. Anyhow," the mother went on, "That's what he says."

"What do you think?" the man asked.

"I think something has been omitted from this equation," the woman stated thoughtfully.

"Ha!" her husband retorted. "Expressing yourself in mathematical terms." He paused to reflect. "Why don't we try another approach? Why don't you meet with Pat's history teacher. Maybe there *is* an element we're overlooking."

A week later, the two parents sat down again to discuss their child.

"I met with Mrs. Cambry. A delightful person."

"Well, she knew you weren't an irate parent coming to blame her for your child's lousy work," Mr. Cummings inserted.

"No, I just think she's nice. Anyhow, she said history isn't just a conglomeration of facts to be memorized. She doesn't teach that way. She emphasizes causes, how they accumulate, compound each other, and the short- and long-term effects of incidents. She showed me the tests Pat took. Every question dealt with the "why" of situations, how they might have evolved in other ways, how they lay the foundation for the next set of events, how seemingly unrelated happenings were in reality connected to each other. Most important, and there it was right in the test, were questions about how we can use the past to help us resolve issues of our own time."

"And Pat is an A student," the father added.

"Right," his wife agreed.

"And the subject goes beyond just concrete facts and figures."

"Yes." Mrs. Cummings thought she knew where her husband was headed but waited for him to make his point.

"And what do you deal with if you're thinking beyond the concrete?" he asked.

"Abstractions," she said smiling.

"Sure. Maybe they're not exactly the same but they're in the same ballpark. Then why can't she do math?"

Pat's parents had now discarded their earlier thinking and some generally accepted but unfounded assumptions about history—how it is taught and its usefulness—and equally unfounded assumptions about why adolescent boys statistically surpass girls in science and mathematics. Cultural influences determine many careers, but as a parent, you should seek to understand your own child as an individual and ignore inapplicable statistics and unproven assertions.

Sometimes a teacher detects a negative pattern being reinforced and takes immediate steps to alter the course of the student's efforts.

"Yes, Liz, you slipped on that exam, in fact, rather badly. But we both know you are capable of much better work, so don't judge yourself by this one test. I certainly won't. As soon as you can find some time, go back over your notes, carefully. See if you can find where you went wrong.

"Maybe you left something out or didn't understand an important step. This subject, you know, is a continuum. If you break one link in the chain, you're in desperate straits.

"Check your textbook to be sure you understand all of the earlier information. I'm fairly sure you'll find a weak area that is correctable. It'll take some extra work, but you'll catch up. Don't forget, if you need help, I'm right here."

Even the best teachers, however, no matter how skilled and dedicated, can't focus on large numbers of individual students. Underachievers usually do not fail in terms of nonpassing grades.

They fail to reach their ability level. Teachers, by the nature of the school program, must concentrate on their classes as a whole unit, and with whatever time remains, should there be any, they attempt to help students falling below the minimal requirements. Underachievers, again, fall between the slats.

You have to help your teenager, just as Pat's parents helped her. After looking as carefully as they could at Pat's efforts, they decided to dismiss the vague explanations of her lack of suitable progress in specific areas. They spoke with her without recriminations or threats or harshness of any kind. Sometimes Pat was annoyed at their "interference" and accused them of "not understanding." Then they then backed off and waited for another opportunity. They patiently explained that parents, trying to assist their children, were not interfering. The role of the parent was to help the child develop so that she could enter the adult world prepared and well adjusted. "Won't you do the same for your own children?"

Pat didn't accept her parents' position immediately, but later brought some homework problems to them for assistance. The trust that they had endeavored to foster in the earlier years now bore fruit. In Pat's thinking, they ceased to be interfering parents and became, rather, knowledgeable adults interested in her welfare. As Pat talked informally with her mother and father and told of school events, most pleasant but some otherwise, they pieced together the missing item in the equation Mrs. Cummings had sought.

Pat's weakness seemed to be an inability to get off to a good start in some subjects, although she hit the ground running in others. Her early performances were based on past experiences, some positive, some otherwise. Pat was able to identify some of these but not all. She repressed most of the negative memories but could recount the opposite type in detail. She proudly related how she questioned her seventh-grade teacher, who spoke of the Indians massacring Custer and the Seventh Cavalry.

"Shouldn't you call that a battlefield victory for the Indians rather than a massacre? After all, wasn't there a treaty recognizing the land as theirs and wasn't it Custer who was doing the invading?"

The teacher hesitated as she pondered Pat's observations and, with an acknowledging wink at Pat, went on, "As I was saying, Sitting Bull and Crazy Horse led their warriors to a brilliant victory over General George Armstrong Custer's outnumbered but highly trained forces. What can we learn from this Indian victory?"

Pat came to understand that her inability to perform at her highest level in certain areas was due to some unfortunate experiences in the past. She had, she realized, developed a fear of some subjects that eventually became an impediment to learning. By thinking about her thinking and her feelings, which she could now do efficiently, she discovered the source of her difficulty. The anxieties she felt were triggered by specific unfavorable incidents, and this emotional response reined in her intellectual ability to cope with these subjects at a high level of performance.

With time and parental patience, Pat began to turn her weak grades around. By the end of the semester, she had only one grade in a major subject below a B, and the course wasn't mathematics. She learned that irrespective of what others do, she must make a greater effort early on in some subjects. She must avoid slow starts. Pat became an Honor Roll student the next semester and never again fell below a B in a major subject, even in those disciplines requiring "abstract thought" and "symbolic manipulations."

The fear of failing, despite earlier negative reinforcement, gradually faded from Pat's attitude, although the original cause or causes were never specifically identified. With parental help and cooperative teachers she built the confidence she needed to master the subjects offered in her school. She understood that sometimes she would have to make an extra effort and that on occasion she would not perform according to her own expectations. She and her cognitive and affective selves "regrouped" and, more heavily armed than earlier, accepted the challenge. The more she succeeded, the easier it became to overcome impediments. She advised her younger sister when hitting a wall to "fall back, look things over, plan, prepare, and go for it."

Expanding Patricia's Advice

The lesson learned and the advice espoused by Pat Cummings should be adopted in some form by all parents to pass on to their underachieving children. But why just the underachievers? Doesn't it pertain to everyone? The answer is yes, but one of the major causes of underachievement in adolescence is a setback in a school or out-of-school event that affects the youth so drastically that she becomes indifferent to scholastic success.

There are other causes of underachievement, as this work submits, but there isn't one remediation plan that works for all. When an overriding disappointment has occurred, and to the teenager that can include any disruption of the expected chain of anticipated events, adolescents tend to overreact. In so doing, one element out of many is boosted above the rest and becomes an issue of paramount importance. The teenager, overly sensitive to begin with, may inflate a rejection, or a slur, real or imagined, into a catastrophe. Remember that a child of this age is usually capable of understanding innuendoes, double entendres, and half-concealed barbs. At this age, she hears with comprehension.

The adolescent may overreact to a low score on a test, a failure to be chosen for a desired group, or lack of an invitation by a peer. The bumper sticker says, in not too polite language, that bad things happen. They do and frequently. The adult doesn't like to be shortchanged at the register, jostled in the crowd, or provided with the wrong merchandise in an order. These are annoyances, but not life-altering events, and reasonably well-adjusted grown-ups throw off the momentary irritation and continue on with more important tasks. They've been there before. The teenager, uncertain of appropriate responses, unsure of herself, and inexperienced, may convert a nuisance into a life-shattering episode:

"Did you hear what he said about me?"

"I get blamed for everything."

"If someone is going to be picked on, it's me."

"My life is ruined."

Slam goes the bedroom door. On goes the stereo—loud. The bedroom is the safe cocoon, protection from the onslaughts of this horrible world.

Setbacks come in all degrees of importance and in all areas of human endeavor. Most, like tropical storms, howl, swirl, and threaten to become hurricanes but blow themselves out without incurring sizable damage and are quickly forgotten. Most of the problems of the teenager blow away like a storm—but not all.

An unfortunate confluence of problems can erode the structures of the affect in the young person, which, in turn, directly interferes with or fails to support healthy cognitive functioning. A blow to an already-existing wound compounds the pain and may have long-term deleterious effects. The well-adjusted adult tells herself, "This too will pass away." The inexperienced adolescent tells herself, "It's all over. There is nothing worth living for."

The wound may manifest itself in any number of ways, but a common one is a letdown in scholarship. "Why exert myself for a meaningless enterprise. School won't help my life. There is nothing in it for me." Cognition becomes limited by dispirited emotions. The innate curiosity of the learner has become unfocused, the motivation dissipated.

Wrap-Up

A major cause of underachievement is an experience or series of experiences that convince the student that he lacks the essential ingredients for success. Therefore, the learner himself may impair his own efforts to overcome failures and weaken his attempts to win when faced with new challenges. All people adopt a system of adjusting to obstructions in their path but not necessarily beneficial ones. A child may learn to blame others or blame the fates for unfair treatment. Should his parents confirm his feelings, he is apt to suspend his efforts too often, and too soon. Somebody or something is hindering him; he doesn't have a chance.

The learner's experiences and attitudes influence his personal expectations, and, if these are limited, his performance will suffer accordingly.

The parental role in dealing with an adolescent is to acknowledge that the learner may need skill development in some areas and may have been the victim of someone's error in the past. However, neither fact is unusual; achievers have to work at sharpening their abilities too. They also may have suffered from someone's gaffe. Furthermore, such episodes may be repeated in the future. The only answer, the learner must understand, is to examine each incident objectively, determine elements that could be improved, and pursue the goal again with more preparation and a greater effort.

16

The Final Wrap-Up

Parents must decide whether a formalized family conference, following a strict schedule and procedural rules, is suitable for the individual in question. Larger families can probably benefit from a preset organizational system as a means of assembling eligible members who might otherwise make independent plans. For example, eighteen-year-old Sue has accepted a tennis date and must leave early, or Dad must prepare his report, which is due the next day. If the meetings are approached as "merely" a family dinner in which some discussions might take place, some participants would be no-shows and others would be able to attend only abbreviated conferences. A loose confederation of family members is apt to be too loose for most get-togethers, thereby defeating the intended purposes.

At the other end of the spectrum, in terms of family size, a single parent and one adolescent underachiever will likely find the idea of a formalized meeting to be ludicrous. Meetings of opportunity, when both have some free time, or when a particular problem arises, or when a news item overshadows all else in the world, may be sufficient for the desired purposes. Each parent must examine the personal circumstances under which the goals of a family roundtable may be met and arrange their conferences accordingly.

The number of participants may be expanded by inviting grandparents, aunts, uncles, and close family friends or neighbors. The personalities of the individuals must be considered with care. Uncle Joe might consider himself to be the family maven and attempt to dominate every meeting. Aunt Sarah may contribute nothing but negatives and curb any enthusiasm the youngster feels. Lionel, the lawyer, ordinarily an interesting and helpful friend, may vie with Uncle Joe for a leadership position and ignore the purposes of the meeting. Before inviting others, the parent must do some serious thinking.

Preadolescent children may be allowed to join the meeting if they do not interrupt its flow. "The child should be seen and not heard" concept is not totally applicable, nor should it be totally rejected either. A ten-year-old may proffer a thought and all members should listen carefully, but some children will tend, if encouraged, to monopolize the conversation with extraneous information. "I saw this neat television program and Slade the Slaughterer hits all the mean guys with his paralysis gun and . . ." Some curbing of the child's input may be necessary.

As a variation, or to increase the number, parents may invite a guest participant who either has some special understanding of the subject to be discussed or merely plays a role similar to the other members. The meetings have maturational and educational purposes, and, if the goals are to be met, possible contributions from each participant become important.

The adolescent is being welcomed and introduced into the world of thinking grown-ups. Many religions and cultures have symbolic rites to recognize the individual as leaving the world of childhood and entering the adult world. The family roundtable, however, is ongoing and directed toward exercising the teenager's abilities to reinterpret the world in terms of his developing mental structures.

The discussions begin with the young person's current interests and branch out in any direction the group finds interesting. The major goal is on the table—the substantive improvement of the student's scholastic performance. The practice in logical thinking and the recognition of emotions in decision making become broad in nature and form an intricate part of the adolescent's system of fact collection, analyses, determinations, and plans for implementation. The mechanisms developed during these discussions are transferrable to most situations, certainly schoolwork.

Ideally, the teenager himself will discover the excitement of learning and the importance of education in his life. Realistically, the parent may have to guide him in this direction from time to time. The task is made easier by his natural entrance into formal operations and the thought-provoking discussions of the roundtable.

All of the remedial efforts aimed at reversing underachievement are centered around the newly developing individual who is leaving childhood. The recognition by the parent of this change in thinking is facilitated by an updated and far more accurate view of adolescents than previously grasped. The parent need never achieve expertise, especially since many claiming to be experts are often not familiar with current investigations and understandings of the adolescent psyche.

Parental requirements for this program do not include a mastery of theory. All you need is a willingness to help your offspring become an achiever. Certainly, some thought is necessary, but this effort is mainly directed toward tailoring the program to the specific needs of your child. Most parents want to be close to their children, and most children want to reciprocate with feelings of love and respect. This approach does not intend for parents to dictate the unfolding of events of their youngster's life or to impose decisions upon him. It does encourage parents to teach children the values they themselves profess and the techniques for learning, applying information and experience to schoolwork and everyday life.

Punishment

Imposing penalties for failure to produce reasonable academic work based on native intelligence is not prohibited in this scheme, but they are not the means to a successful outcome either. Punishment, such as the deprivation of privileges, is an acceptable approach to misbehaving children. When used as a means to foster improved schoolwork with adolescents, its use becomes questionable. Each parent knows her own youngster. If parents are chastising and disciplining work, then they might use punishment as a means to correct offenses. But is lack of effort in school the same as mischievous behavior or disregarding important parental regulations?

Punishment is decidedly a negative action. Think about it. The parent is trying to instill a love and appreciation of the benefits of learning in her child. Is it sensible then for the young person to associate negativity with education? It's not likely that you would be reading this book if merely "grounding" or similar disciplinary measures had made an achiever out of your child. Rats can be taught to avoid shocks by not walking on an electric grid, but that type of learning is not transferrable to other situations. Your goal is to have your teenager, at his new level of readiness, conclude that learning is in his best interest. You want him to study, not to please you or because he's afraid of being punished, but because he realizes that his efforts will result in a better life, now and later.

A more subtle kind of punishment, provided indirectly, is probably more effective for most youngsters. Utilize some kind of reward system. Cooperation by your child in an effort to upgrade his marks by listening more carefully in school, by doing his homework thoroughly and on time, and by preparing thoroughly for tests should be rewarded. This could take the form of a special present (the tennis racket he wanted), an extra unit of freedom (an extended curfew), or a dinner at his favorite restaurant. Higher test scores followed by an improved report card might call for greater rewards.

Some purists could argue that rewards offered, but subsequently not earned, are tantamount to punishment for not meeting his obligation. Not many adolescents will feel that way. Instead, the tendency will be for the youngster to associate good effort with parental approval and that indefinable feeling of satisfaction—the intrinsic reward—when he finally hits the target.

Reassurance

The defendant, as he finishes responding to the prosecuting attorney's series of rapid-fire questions, looks toward his own lawyer. She sits there looking back at him and nods. Relieved, the accused feels the relaxation in his abdomen and, a bit more confident, turns toward his tormentor, who has reloaded and is preparing to fire again. Suppose the defense counsel had averted eye contact by looking away? That would have signaled him: he had blown it; the case was lost and he was prison bound.

The twelve-year-old stumbles over her lines, but the audience waits patiently for her to continue with the play. She looks toward Mr. Feen, her teacher, who smiles approvingly. Assured that there has been no disaster, she continues, and performs even better than at the rehearsal.

Parents, too, must render reassurance when needed, and this help may be no more than an approval sign at the right time. Without speaking a word, a comforting message can still be transmitted. "You are all right. I'm with you. Keep going." The parental role is to build confidence, which makes success possible and prepares the groundwork for more success.

Logic versus Emotion

One of the supreme human errors is the assumption that logic will overcome strong emotions. Logic can win the field only when the affective view is passive or only mildly involved. Students, for instance, learning about the civilization of the Aztecs are not predisposed to reject the achievements of that historical people. Few students would have personal objections about admiring a people alive only in books. Sure. Respect their accomplishments. Why not?

Tell a devout conservative that change, a fundamental law of nature, is inexorable and he'll agree, providing that you omit his cherished beliefs. Tell an unrelenting liberal that reality must be recognized as it exists and not as he wishes it to be, and he, too, will concur until his ideals are challenged. In these and innumerable other areas, logic loses its vigor when cast against proverbial immovable objects such as petrified belief systems bolstered by strong emotions.

How about your adolescent underachiever? Reasonable explanations may change his attitude if the emotional aspects involved are relatively minor. If his feelings about an item are strong and diametrically opposed to your position, your argument, no matter how forceful, will be impotent.

The ascendancy of emotion over cognition occurs constantly in everyday life. Politicians and ideologists find slogans more persuasive than reason, no matter how compelling that reason may be.

"I'll introduce legislation calling for a new retirement system for all Americans that will make those golden years truly pleasurable." *Yes.*

"I'll guarantee not only that taxes will not be increased, they'll be cut!" *Yes.*

"How am I going to do that? I'll cut out the waste and needless expenditures. Are you going to tell me that tax money has never been wasted? Are you going to tell me that in that huge budget, nothing can be reduced? Nonsense!" Yes, nonsense.

When an emotion is solidified, hard facts will make little impression.

"I know that air is the safest way to travel, but I'm still anxious."

"I know nothing happens in crowded elevators, but I still feel like screaming."

Even when the emotion is not a phobia, if it has strong roots, such as prejudice, it will resist reason.

The formal schooling of a youngster cannot be separated effectively from the emotional side of his life. Educators have always recognized the importance of the affect in learning but have treated it as a supportive state, whereas in reality, it permeates every aspect of learning.

The student preparing for a homework assignment, if properly trained, will collect his tools, information, and other necessities before starting. He knows, by an accepted thought-out process, that efficiency will save him considerable time and effort and yield desirable results. Utilizing an established procedure with his materials at hand, he moves expeditiously to the heart of the assignment. "What do I have to do?" he asks himself. He knows that reading a column just now on that sports page will cost him valuable time and that seeing his brother passing by doesn't mean that this is a propitious moment to discuss borrowing his Walkman. Focus on the task at hand, the affect commands. In this case, the thinking and the feeling are working in cooperation.

The emotional side, however, is playing a vital role. The student is confident of his ability to do the assignment well in a short period of time. He feels secure in the knowledge that all of the information and processing techniques required for this job are at his disposal. He combines his feelings of adequacy and his interest in the topic to solve the problems in the assignment.

However, the student whose feelings have not been synchronized with his cognitive ability may view the challenge as too great, perhaps overwhelming. His self-effacing approach may be reinforced by the experience of other failures in his past. He has the capability to work at this level in terms of his thinking processes, but he can't overcome the impinging negative emotions. Who needs this stuff, anyway? It's stupid.

Schools, tutors, and learning centers focus on the subject at hand and attempt to impart enough knowledge to help the learner bridge the chasm between his current level and the school's requirements. The underachiever may need the material provided, but the cause of his learning deficit may remain untouched. Quite likely, the student, from a long-term view, is worse off. The special treatment may, at times, breach an obvious obstacle. The learner, however, not being motivated to master the material in the first place, is now up to date in content but tired of, bored with, and perhaps antagonistic toward the subject. The remedy may be symptomatic, temporary, and counterproductive. This student's performance level is quite likely to sink again. He needs long-term remediation.

Parental expectations and parental worries have a profound, if hidden, impact on the maturing mind of the teenager. Parental thoughts, not always expressed orally, are being read and interpreted by the adolescent and may assist or hinder his development. Outside forces are offering constant stimuli not only to this semi-adult but to the parents too. Among these influences is television, which helps to shape the opinions of viewers in many subjects, sometimes by portraying events with singular accuracy and sometimes with ideological distortions. The adolescent, trying to find his place in the environment, and at an impressionable period in life, tends to believe much of what he is shown. Adults, although hardened by negative experiences, tend to be skeptical, but they, too, may overreact when their children are the subject.

One book such as this cannot illustrate the myriad of possible examples that may cause a needless upset, but let's look at a typical one. Remember, your actions concerning your child send out invisible signals to that inquiring mind. You want those signals to be helpful.

An Imaginary Conversation

"We need something to put life into the six o'clock news. The mayor has the approval for the new budget, nothing is happening in the state capital, and no one is running for office right now."

"How about a series on those weapons that high school kids are carrying to school?"

"That would be good but I just had lunch with Harry. Channel 13 has been preparing a special on that and they're announcing it tonight."

"I see where the Johnson kid killed himself. How about something like that?"

"Teenage suicide?"

"Right."

"What's happening with the statistics?"

"The rate is climbing."

"Oh. Well, let's look into it. Check on the last time we or the competition reported on it. Line up some parents who have experienced this kind of tragedy and some psychiatrists who deal with it. See if we can give it a new slant, you know, like telltale signs of impending disaster."

Checking It Out

"My child is a teenager now and I'm scared to death," the obviously upset mother, Estelle Wilbert, explains.

"What has she done to cause this alarm?" the therapist asks.

"Oh, lots of things. All the time."

"Give me an illustration. Pick one or two recent events and tell me about them."

"Well, I can't right now. It's not so much what she's done but what she might do."

"What might she do?" the therapist asks patiently.

"Any number of things, like suicide. Yes, like suicide."

"Okay. Let's talk about that. Give me some of the facts. Tell me about her actions recently and whatever she's said that's causing this concern."

"Well, she hasn't done anything, exactly. Or said anything. But she's at that age. I saw this special on television and the rate of suicide among teenagers is increasing."

The therapist watches Mrs. Wilbert's facial expressions and stares at her eyes. "Tell me if I'm missing something. Your daughter isn't showing signs of being suicidal or being depressed or expressing something specific that is causing you to worry. You're concerned about what you've seen on television. Right?"

"I guess so. The only sign I can think of is that she hasn't been doing well in school. She was a good student, but from A's and B's she's fallen to mostly C's."

The therapist hesitates, then asks, "How does she react to these lower grades?"

"She doesn't seem to care. If anything, she's more concerned about their effect on me than anything else. By the way, speaking of depression, she came home one afternoon last week and ran into her bedroom. I could hear her crying until she raised the volume on her stereo."

"How long did that last?" the therapist inquires.

"At least until dinnertime," the mother answers seriously and, noticing the therapist's grin, joins him in laughter. "Depression, indeed," she says snatching the words away from him. "You're going to tell me it's like hearing about a disease and then imagining you have the symptoms. Right?"

Life-Threatening Behavior Can Be Real

The problems of adolescents using illegal drugs, running away, committing felonies, and attempting suicide are very real and a concern to society in general. Any parent facing such possibilities in her teenager needs to take immediate steps to remedy the cause, consider professional help, and act quickly to prevent a tragedy.

Many teenagers at some time consider suicide. Statistics in this area should not be of concern to parents unless their adolescent also displays questionable or specific suicidal tendencies. The numbers game of those who have "considered" taking their own lives reveals little. There is a vast difference between considering and actually attempting suicide. Although the rate of suicide among youngsters has risen, the percentage of such attempts among adolescents remains low. A greater threat to the life of a teenager is posed by accidents. Also, one must consider the suicide rate among adults, which is relatively high. Some fifty to seventy thousand people kill themselves yearly. How many more deaths resulting from people taking their own lives who are listed in some other category is speculative. The number of adults who "considered" this act is also vague. But the popularity of written materials on ways to make a final exit and the use of suicide machines is self-evident. The problem, then, is of import to all of society. It isn't just a teenage concern but relates to the general population.

The concerned parent frequently asks, "Are sex acts and possibly pregnancy petty misbehavior?" Most parents decry such behavior, but society is changing rapidly and sexual activity is part of that change. The problem was not created by profligate teenagers but by adults who buy the books and the movie tickets and watch the television programs that feature promiscuous sex. The "liberated" sexual activity concept started with adults who equated the "pill" with permissiveness, discarded traditional restraints, and, thus, transformed society. Today's adolescents are following the path paved by their progenitors.

You, the parent, unless you have indications that your child is behaving in some aberrant fashion, should concentrate on his poor scholarship. Schools may not be able to adjust to the changes in society and provide for today's needs, but you can have a favorable impact both scholastically and morally.

Your adolescent lives in the nineties and is hardly isolated from society. Your child not only watches television and can read, he understands. Fundamentally, he is like teenagers in the past, but his views are current and, in many cases, more advanced than his parents. Unlike his younger years, he knows he may not always be right. In middle childhood, he often took issue with his parents about items that affected him directly but frequently sensed that he might be wrong. Now as a teenager, he may take issue with his parents about items that affect him directly and about items that are general, but the new cognitive element is in place and operating. Your teenager can think about what he is thinking; he can analyze his own thoughts, criticize his own views, and modify his position. He has the capability of stepping back from himself to examine his own reflections in a very objective way.

The ability to self-evaluate differs by age, experience, and individual genetic factors. Some children are already thinking in a high order at age eleven, whereas some adults—in fact, many of them—never reach this plane. If your child has open-minded parents who serve as role models, your teenager will rapidly develop the mental structures necessary for adult learning and the application of this knowledge.

His developing intellect arouses intense curiosity in areas previously shrouded and also bestows upon him the authority to try things on his own. He has, he feels, by virtue of his maturation, the inherent right to go places without his parents' permission and often without his parents' knowledge. Fortunately, there are two edges to his sharpened intellect. The world unfolding before him has indeed aroused his curiosity, which serves as an impetus for exploration, but on the other side of the blade is the ability to comprehend the consequences of his actions. His view now includes all of the possible outcomes of an act, which, in the case of nonconforming behavior, almost always serves as a restraining mechanism.

With these psychological changes clearly in mind, you can form a more accurate and comprehensive view of his likely behavior. You are now ready to initiate specific measures aimed at improving his scholarship.

The program, if implemented correctly, is designed to place an informed parent in the role of presenting opportunities to the learner to uproot the causes of his educational and related problems and develop the qualities necessary for scholarship and adjustment.

Expectations

Interspersed throughout this work there is a direct and implied reference to the effect of expectations of others on the student. Their views may be particularly discouraging to an adolescent who is trying to fit in somewhere, who is vulnerable to positive and negative suggestions and affected by remarks, especially ones that are demeaning. When emotions are involved, facts and logic retreat to a back burner.

A distraught mother tried to describe the event that had precipitated her family "crisis." Her gesticulation seemed aimless, her unfinished sentences puzzling, and her discomfiture was unsettling to the listener—me.

"Now Mrs. Vinelli, why don't you just stop for a moment. Sit back. Let all those thoughts trying to get out simultaneously go back where they came from. Put them into some sort of order in your mind."

The parent settled back into the chair and half smiled. "Relax, right? Start at the beginning?" Mrs. Vinelli nodded as if I had offered the instructions.

"No," I countered. "You're not going to relax until you've established some mode of communication with me. That will come. But don't start at the beginning, at least not yet. Think for a bit and summarize the problem in one sentence if you can."

"Well, we became aware of the problem last Friday . . ."

"Hold it. No details yet. No thoughts about the problem. Just tell me what the problem is."

"It's Mike, my son. He thinks he's not smart enough to go to college."

I reached for my pad and a pen, not to take notes, but to conceal my annoyance over the parent's emotional involvement in a routine decision-making situation.

Either Mrs. Vinelli had well-developed ESP or I had failed to conceal my reaction to her concern, because her attitude changed.

"It's a big problem in our family. You said no details. One sentence. Don't write it off so cavalierly."

I stood naked in the window. Thus exposed, I sought refuge in a classical but effective escape. I apologized.

My admission of a mistake had a salutary effect on the woman and she proceeded to tell her story, succinctly and with details. I forgot about my pad and pen and listened intently. You can't deal with a problem until you have identified it. This woman had to communicate the problem to me, and there is no communication without a listener. I believe the theories I espouse.

Mrs. Vinelli's problem, in various versions, is common among parents with adolescent children. The parents were eager to have their son attain the highest level of education possible for him. They knew there had to be an upper limit, but certainly, in their view, a high school diploma wasn't it. Mike, they realized in his early years, was capable of at least one college degree and a professional-type career. Both of the Vinelli's had come from households where well-developed hand skills, hard work, and perseverance accounted for comfortable family incomes. Mike's grandparents on both sides were proud, honest, family-oriented people who considered themselves an integral part of the nation's spine. But shouldn't a young man strive, as the Army says, "to be all that he can be?" If he can work with his brain, shouldn't he pursue a career requiring knowledge and mental skills? The Vinelli's decided the answer was clearly affirmative and talked about college to Mike as early as his primary grades. They were always interested in his schooling, actively cooperated with his school, helped him develop a discipline for doing homework, and encouraged learning whenever possible. And they did more.

The Vinelli's budgeted carefully so that educational funds were set aside for Mike and his two younger sisters. Mike, while attending college, might have to work for his spending money, but his tuition, fees, and books would be paid for by the family. He would graduate without debt and be free to pursue his chosen career.

Mike was a good student throughout his first eight years of school, and his parents never considered the possibility that he wasn't college material. Now, at age fourteen, the youngster had "discovered" he didn't have the innate mental capacity to earn a college degree.

Etiology of a Problem

The teacher in Mike's American history class is called to the hallway by a vice principal who requires some urgent information.

Sheila, a student seated near the teacher's desk, notices his role book is open and decides to see if the marks of a recent test, as yet unreturned, are recorded. What she sees are I.Q.'s after each student's name. She determines her own, then glances at others near hers. "Mike, you've got the lowest. Only 108. Mine is 122 and Jack has 119. Mike, I thought you were smarter than that."

Mike, on returning home from school that day, goes straight to his room. He doesn't want dinner, he doesn't want to talk, he wants to be let alone. Later, he tells his mother of his findings. Forget college. He doesn't want to go to college anyway. "It's your goal, not mine," he tells his mother. That night she hears his muffled sobs as he cries away his mother's dream.

Multiple Perceptions

The academic success of your child depends on how he is perceived by the school, by his peers, by you, and by himself. Each estimate of his potential becomes an important element in the forces impinging on him, and together they affect his academic, athletic, and social performances. Perceptions vary from the same sources, depending on the skill in question. Many parents have heard a teacher say, "He's not an outstanding student, but he's such a nice boy." The football coach may not care about grades as long as they're high enough to keep the player on the team.

"I know you won an award for writing a composition. That's great. But on this team when the quarterback is in trouble, you change your pass-catching pattern and run back toward him! Got it?" A psychologically trained, informed coach would have added the words "I know you can do it."

The elements comprising self-perception are the most vital of all, but this view frequently reflects the evaluations expressed by others. Sometimes, only one statement is enough to change behavior and remain in the conscious mind throughout a lifetime. Remember the story of the sandlot game and the center fielder whose disparaging act of leaving his position and coming to the infield could have shattered the batter emotionally? He never forgot. Another case involved a fifteen-year-old girl who, overcoming some reluctance, asked a boy to a dance. Within hearing distance of some other teenagers, and using a raised voice with feigned shock, he exclaimed, "I wouldn't go out with anyone as ugly as you." The law doesn't recognize words as sufficient cause for violence, but if her father had been there the boy might never had gone out with anyone, ever.

The Process of Adjusting

Evaluative statements do shape the behavior of people no matter how couched, but parents cannot always be there to shield their children from thorns. They can, to some extent, build insulation by showing interest and giving appropriate reassurances. Mrs. Wilbert and Mrs. Vinelli overreacted in their fears about adolescents and in their expectations for their children, but remember that parental concern is like nothing else on earth. A father of two boys under ten asked, "When do you stop worrying about your kids?" The answer is, never.

This work has devoted special attention to the thinking and behavior of the adolescent underachiever. The underachiever, however, is not a separate being. She's still an adolescent. Earlier, for instance, we described the commonly observed adolescent approach to disquieting events—self-exile to her room. Parental efforts to thwart this action are ill conceived. The youngster may come bursting through the door from the outside and, breaking all speed limits, head for the bedroom or, in the middle of an argument or even a discussion with a parent, suddenly break off the discourse and head for privacy. To disturb this procedure is to light a match in a gas-filled confined space. The adolescent has smashed up against a seemingly impenetrable barrier while her cylinders continue to pump at maximum speed. The problem could be in her social world or in her home life. The emotional state has taken over, and she wouldn't recognize a cognitive solution if it were painted on a wall in front of her. She is confronting danger, and although mental, not physical, she employs the ageless method of salvation—escape. Off to the bedroom.

"I don't know what I'm going to do with her," implore many parents. You should do nothing at the moment. The action of the adolescent is merely a way to extricate herself from a situation that she sees as intimidating or even menacing. First, she must free herself from the immediate circumstances of her plight, and then she must find safe haven while she decides how to manage an unpalatable event. Her bedroom is her refuge. She can shut out the outside world and, unlike Humpty Dumpty, put the pieces back together again. The loud music, preferably with a distinct beat, not only shields her from the "enemy" but helps to overpower her own surging emotions. She becomes caught up in the rhythm of the stereo, which suppresses the affairs she is not ready to face and allows her to engage in some harmless fantasies.

This action taken by the teenager, a catharsis of sorts, is not limited to the adolescent years. Adults do similar things to "let off steam." They may throw the nearest object, perhaps a vase, even though it wasn't designed to be a missile, or go for a brisk walk or scrub the kitchen floor. The latter two, obviously, are favorable alternatives. One can observe the attempted release of frustration every workday by watching drivers leaving work and heading for home who change lanes constantly, although there is no opening in the traffic, who drive excessively fast only to screech to a stop at the next light, who utilize horns needlessly, and who attack fellow drivers with obscene gestures bathed in triple-X language. The recipient of their attacks appears to be the motorist who didn't start moving in anticipation of a green light or who didn't appreciate being cut off at a turn. The real target is the fathead boss who obtained his position the same way he was conceived—by accident, the sure sale that choked to death moments before the papers were signed, or the endless boredom of sameness day after day. The adolescent who sequesters herself from time to time is not avoiding reality in a serious sense. She is regrouping. In a short time or even overnight, if necessary, she returns to her normal self, a pain in the derriere. But you love her.

A typical fallback position of humans is the act of blaming

others for ineffectual efforts on their own part. Adolescents, in an outburst, may shift the fault of failure or poor work toward someone else. The teacher may have made a mistake, the parent failed to help, the friend didn't do her part. All of these accusations may have elements of truth, but the teenager usually grasps the real picture. Others may have played a role in her stumbling, but she alone is responsible for her own actions and must take the responsibility. In her current stage of mental development she is able to evaluate her own actions with a fair degree of objectivity.

The informed parent recognizes normal adolescent behavior and the possible reasons for it. She must wait until the young person is ready to discuss the problem. The process of "putting things into perspective" is a good topic for the family roundtable.

Looking Ahead

After you, the parent, have set in motion a series of remedial efforts using your child's natural developing characteristics to reinforce his learning techniques and to set procedures in place to overcome failures, you may do some reevaluating of previously held notions. Return to the early profile you drew, update where necessary, and look forward to a not-too-distant future evaluation.

Look at the general characteristics of an achiever. Determine those that have already been acquired by your child and decide which of the remaining categories require further attention. Few people will be outstanding in every measurement, but you decide, for your child as an individual, which have been achieved and which are realistically within reach of attainment. Dream anything you wish, but reach for the possible.

Profiles

The organization of your impressions about your child's characteristics should have provided clues to his ability, special talents, and needs. As you proceed with the program, your views are likely to undergo revision. Some strengths, hardly suspected, might be uncovered, and some weak areas may prove not to be innate but experienced based. The program should alter the unwanted effects of past experiences.

Initial profiles, in many cases, are based on superficial and even snap judgments. Later versions of profiles tend to differ because of three factors:

1. The parent, now armed with a better understanding of adolescents, is considering every word more carefully. Certainty is out; caution is in.
2. The youngster, now in the formal operations stage, is undergoing a natural change. Even if the parent did nothing, some of this mental development would still occur.
3. The recommended program, followed in any version, or done in part, has a role in reshaping the characteristics of the teenager.

A psychological profile, prepared by a professional, would provide more volume and possible explanations for underachievement. The parent, however, is not seeking bulk but rather a concise reading of her child that might offer some possible revelations. If the process of filling out the profile and returning to it later provides one helpful clue, the effort has paid a dividend. In the sample cases offered, there were substantial payoffs.

The final version of the profile should list all, or at least many, of the developing characteristics enumerated.

Developing Characteristics

Your teenager is becoming:

- Self-reliant and self-confident. He is working with more enthusiasm, more persistence, and little fear of failure.
- Cognizant of his own capabilities across the spectrum. He is utilizing his strengths for progress but is constantly attempting to fortify his weaknesses.

- Curious. He is open to new interests with an intense desire to learn.
- Flexible and therefore adapts to changing situations, often anticipating change before most other adolescents.
- Aware of his responsibilities and the consequences of his actions for himself and other people.

Your teenager is harvesting the fruits of his imagination as he explores all possibilities in puzzles, tasks, and events. When working on an assignment, he:

- Is a quick starter who determines early the essence of the challenge and the best method in which to proceed.
- Utilizes all of the information available, decides on resources needed and possible assistance.
- Brings past experience to the fore in designing his approach and operates efficiently. He applies techniques that have worked for him in the past.
- Checks his progress as he proceeds and makes modifications of his strategy if necessary.
- Is undaunted by obstacles; he rethinks his understanding of the problem, looks for possible errors, and searches for solutions.
- Knows when he has completed the task and evaluates his efforts.

An Achiever's View

Competition. The young person reaching maturity is entering a world pleading for fresh ideas, effective innovations, creativity, and problem-solving approaches. Developed talent is the new gold sought by commerce, industry, universities, and government. Opportunities abound as never before in a world of constant transition. The person prepared in training, self-discipline, and sharp thinking abilities at his optimal level has minimal competition.

Success. Success is personal fulfillment. It means reaching for goals that change as an individual approaches them. From his own perspective a person is never successful, irrespective of wealth, status, and work enjoyment, unless he is always pursuing his dream in some intelligent fashion.

Addendum

Some parents feel, on reviewing segments of the manuscript, that some unusual slants and further explanations of covered material should be included in the body of the text. The author feels, however, that either all major topics have been discussed, or else they are not directly a part of the remedial program for underachievers.

Other matters, unless explained adequately, may be ambiguous and misleading. These subjects, therefore, are included in this section as responses to actual parental questions.

PARENT: I'm not clear on the I.Q. The test does or doesn't measure intelligence?

WRITER: The I.Q. test measures certain aspects of intelligence, especially the kind that is useful in a formal school setting. That is precisely the reason for its existence. The results, however, do not provide an estimate of all abilities, and some of these may be very instrumental in determining the achievement of a person.

PARENT: What is "divergent" intelligence?

WRITER: It's an ill-understood characteristic of human intelligence sometimes equated with creativity. The creativity, however, may not be of the artistic type, although there probably is an overlap. The person with high divergent intelligence sees the world somewhat differently than the great majority. A confusing issue is that all people have some divergent ability, and the same type of characteristic is exhibited by adolescents and people generally considered very bright. The difference is a matter of degree.

The child with a highly divergent intellect is likely to be affected by his atypical mental structures much earlier in life. He probably reaches formal operations long before his peers and then goes much further than they in developing and displaying these behaviors. He lives with this different intelligence throughout life, but not always happily.

PARENT: Why not?

WRITER: If he acts on his inclinations, he may operate in a fashion that is counter to the vast majority. He learns early that derision and ostracism may result from following his compulsions. Many, therefore, curb their feelings and respond to society as society expects.

PARENT: If they let themselves go, they would be considered nonconformists?

WRITER: Yes, but not necessarily in every area.

PARENT: Then what they have isn't a detriment, right? Should a parent encourage divergent thinking?

WRITER: A parent should encourage this ability but help the child understand that others might not see the environment and human relations as he does. His contributions in any field, which could be significant, must be presented in segments with full explanations of why they are justified. He should till the ground before planting the seeds of his ideas.

PARENT: How do I recognize these attributes?

WRITER: First, do not assume that an act of nonconformity or an attack on the establishment necessarily is a demonstration of high divergent intelligence. Just being different in and of itself is not a characteristic. The divergent-thinking person, at any age, tends to:

- Think independently.
- Question the accepted.
- Tie seemingly disparate things together.
- Recognize problems in their embryonic stage.
- Reflect seriously on problems that have no personal effect on him.
- Be compassionate for people needing help.
- Be flexible in most matters.
- Be a dreamer, not of personal glory, but of human progress.

PARENT: I don't see anything unusual about the items on the list.

WRITER: Remember my caution. Everyone has all or most of these qualities built into his mentality. The question is one of intensity. The divergent thinker, if these urges are nurtured, will be the discoverer, the inventor, the planner, or the problem solver. He may work with mechanical appliances or difficult abstractions. If encouraged, he'll produce.

He's not necessarily a leader, but people who are in charge should have some low-profile divergent thinkers in their advisory group.

PARENT: Are there other types who differ from the mainstream who are underachievers because of their difference?

WRITER: There are, of course, those who have been classified as late bloomers. They take longer than most to get it (affective aligned with cognitive, blended with experience) all together. When they do, they match their intellectual equals and sometimes surpass them in performance.

Another type, rarely if ever mentioned in the professional literature or discussed by teachers and psychologists, is the person who hesitates for a significant period of time before acting or even speaking. The pause may be in response to an intellectual question, a routine query, or an assigned manual project.

I came across this early in my teaching career and wondered about it but took no active interest until I observed the same characteristic in a government official. This particular person was chairing the zoning board of a large city and was respected by all who knew him. When it was necessary for him to speak, he seemed to stare into vacant space, expressionless, with all limbs frozen into position. Many people pause before speaking to arrange their ideas into some desired order and to prepare, even if for an instant, some suitable phraseology. I'm not referring to that. The zoning chairperson seemed lifeless for an inordinate amount of time while the audience stirred uncomfortably. The other members of the zoning board, however, seemed to take no notice of the delay, showing absolutely none of the discomfiture of the others in the room. They were familiar with the delivery system of their leader.

When the chairperson began to speak, he delivered in concise terms a complete summary of the proceedings, the arguments for and against a zoning change, and the relevant points of issue the board would consider. Anyone who had missed the meeting and had entered the room only at the time the chairperson began to speak would have been able, if she desired, to write a report of what had transpired for an hour without missing a single important element.

A similar approach to a problem was used by a student staring at a dining room table that was tilting because of a wobbly leg. I happened to be visiting the classroom teacher, and when I entered the room the youngster was already looking at the table. Other students in this woodshop were busily engaged in a variety of activities.

The teacher and I were standing at the front of the room talking about a future conference. I kept glancing at the student, who was still standing looking at the table. After a few more minutes, my curiosity took over.

"What's that kid doing over there? The one looking at the table."

"Fixing it," came the laconic reply. The teacher then continued to present information on the projected conference.

"How's he fixing it, with will power?" I immediately apologized for my sarcasm because this was a competent instructor who inspired adolescents to do their best work. He seemed to take no offense.

"Do you want an explanation before he makes the repair or do you want to wait until the job is done?"

Before I could answer, the student suddenly moved like a master craftsman. In about half the time a skilled worker could have completed the task, he repaired the table.

"Okay, Mr. Morgan, it's done," he reported confidently.

The teacher and I went over to the table and inspected the work. Mr. Morgan nodded approvingly, and I, with unconcealed awe, admired the student's accomplishment. The teacher then offered his explanation, which served as a basis for understanding how some unusual minds function.

Many people, facing a task, dive in as if it were a heated, safe pool ready to welcome them. Others look over the possibilities before selecting the most appropriate process to employ, while still others plan extensively before beginning. None of these methods truly reflect the mental mechanics that take place with the delayed response person (D.R.P.). These people think through each phase of the operation, whether it is a concrete object or an abstraction, down to minute details. Before they begin, their mind has already made the necessary measurements, integrated possibilities, eliminated extraneous movements or information, and anticipated all conceivable problems or objections. Until the entire task has been completed mentally, they refrain from physical action or speaking. When they initiate their efforts, they move or speak with precision until they reach their goals.

As students, these quite competent individuals are likely to be underachievers. A teacher, for example, calls on one of them to list a major cause of World War I. Just one? Most prepared students will offer any of a number they have read and understood. The D.R.P., however, may respond briefly but more often becomes locked into his pattern of processing symbols and reviews all of the causes of the war he has studied, selects from among them, and phrases his answer to fit the question. He wants to get it just right. By this time, the teacher, not knowing if a response is even forthcoming, justifiably calls on someone else. The D.R.P. is perplexed and discouraged. He knew the answer. He was going to give it. What happened?

Many tests are timed and must be completed within a specified period. The D.R.P. has extreme difficulty operating close to his optimal level under pressure from the clock. His mentality is not naturally designed for a classroom.

D.R.P.'s, however, can frequently outperform the competition if they are placed in suitable positions where the work demands competency without time constraints.

PARENT: Some of us question your flat assertion that many of the needs of the underachiever cannot be met by the schools. You categorically assert that "schools can't."

WRITER: Obviously, the educational system cannot provide everything for everyone. Schools must focus on academic training and the development of marketable skills. As shown earlier, much is known of human development that should be incorporated into an educational curriculum. The importance of the affect in learning, recognized but hardly attended to, would require a complete revamping of the educational program. None of this is about to happen while your child can still benefit from possible improvements.

PARENT: What then?

WRITER: Provide it yourself.

PARENT: You seem to take issue with many established recommendations for helping underachievers. Would you clarify your position?

WRITER: Many of the suggestions are not incorrect but are obviously simplistic and fail to reach the base of the problem. Look at some of them. "Set a daily goal." Well, maybe for small children, but not for adolescents. Goals in and of themselves are not sufficient motivators. Just reciting some words, especially those imposed on the youngster by parents, is ineffective. The young person discovers his own goals as he develops his thinking process. Goals must be felt in order to be worthwhile.

Many other recommendations are just as superficial and have no impact on learning, such as setting specific hours for study. The time involved depends on the assignment and the individual. Another almost useless recommendation is to avoid studying after meals. This is invariably associated with a lecture on the process of digestion, the work load of the heart supplying blood, and the possible feeling of tiredness. If some are thus affected, that is, with a loss of energy after a meal, then of course that's the wrong time to study. Relating the obvious to a teenager is self-deflating. He feels that he is either being patronized or considered stupid. These suggestions are unrelated to the serious causes of underachievement.

PARENT: Keep going.

WRITER: Repeat. It's not that the common suggestions of many educators are wrong, it's that an intelligent parent would readily deal with them. Consider having your youngster "avoid distractions," "take breaks away from work," "stretch," "work rapidly," or "suppress intruding thoughts." Again, you're talking to a teenager.

These typical, surface suggestions will not overcome problems. Instead, you must build the infrastructure of learning by supplementing the school's efforts. We've covered the plan. There isn't an item that cannot be done by a parent operating in earnest. With the program digested, a parent can relate to her child in a more sophisticated manner and help him:

- Use his increased self-awareness.
- Use his awareness of others.
- Use his interactions with others and their thinking to broaden his own thoughts.
- Use his understanding of how language enables him to communicate.

PARENT: I get the feeling of an opportunity lost.

WRITER: You're on target. The second half of their school career could be an exciting time for youngsters in a psychological era that understands them as never before. Schools could provide a mechanism for motivation that would have no past precedent. Educational systems reinforced with modern technology that is properly utilized could present knowledge in an ambience specifically designed to promote continuous interest. Teachers, skillfully supported, could not exhaust the possibilities of interesting challenges. They could offer a menu so varied and attractive that every normal teenager would be shoving his intellectual plate forward to receive his share of the goodies.

The teenager is more than a body responding to activated glands. He is a mind stimulated by new thought patterns reaching out to a world he never understood before and finding that he is a part of it. He wants to know how this world works, what it means, and what his role is. As a child he was always curious, but now he is no longer satisfied with any answer. He wants to know how and on what basis the answer was derived. There seem to be endless aspects of living to explore, and he wants to become familiar with all of them. His mind is kinetic energy, vigorous and dynamic, ready and eager to learn. The role of the parent is to open up the blinds and let him look out and wonder.

PARENT: The child entering this stage of formal operations now deals on a different level with society. Right? My kid seems to fit the description you gave but I'm worried about her social life. She isn't very popular. What makes a person popular and does that have anything to do with underachievement?

WRITER: There could be a relationship. People are popular for many reasons that may overlap, but let's list some that you usually find in achievers. The person in question makes a good appearance, is enthusiastic and energetic, has wide interests, may be athletic, is usually friendly and outgoing, is sympathetic, unselfish, nonconfrontational, considerate, and avoids untruths.

Not many people display an abundance of all of these qualities, but if the person has some reasonable quantity of each and perhaps a few that are outstanding, the person will be well liked.

PARENT: And the unpopular characteristics?

WRITER: People who are continually negative, inactive, grudge carriers, quarrelsome, bullies, rude, braggarts, snobs, and overly sensitive are not generally liked.

Schoolwork could easily be affected by the personality factors in each list. That's why I stress awareness of others and self-awareness. It's like looking at yourself in a mirror and seeing only the cognitive and the affect instead of the physical self.

PARENT: My son seems to get excited about some news item and takes it very seriously. He goes beyond a normal concern, I think. What do I do about it?

WRITER: I've said this before, but it keeps coming up so I'll repeat it for emphasis.

Teenagers tend to be idealistic and seekers of justice. They want to restructure society. They are influenced by an "expert" who may only be espousing his own ideology or a ratings-seeking television program. They combine the limitations of children who respond to inadequate evidence and their newly developed mental capacity that allows them to consider multiple explanations and solutions. Thus, they question authority, seek cures for the ills facing humanity, and then opt for simple solutions. In so doing, they tend to confuse themselves. It doesn't matter, however, since they do little themselves to bring about a change and lose interest in a given matter rather quickly.

PARENT: You seem to downplay the perils of adolescence. Hardly a day goes by without some report about high school students carrying weapons, neighborhood violence, or teens involved in some reprehensible activity.

WRITER: You're right on all counts. Remember, though, my qualification. I'm referring to middle-class adolescents and excluding disadvantaged youth, who have very real problems and require society's attention and assistance, and teenagers over the age of fifteen. Serious problems still exist in the remaining group, but the same or similar dilemmas have always existed. The media rarely differentiates between groups by socioeconomic background or even, sometimes, by age. They locate examples, real ones, not fabrications, but their illustrations are not representative of adolescents as a whole and certainly not of a specific age group. The focus of reporters is on the human-interest angle and not on scientific proportions.

PARENT: Are you suggesting that the media be curbed?

WRITER: Only if you wish to end freedom as we know it. Let them report, unintended distortions and all.

PARENT: Then what?

WRITER: Teach high school kids critical thinking and have them employ analytical techniques in their course work. One example, but an important one, will illustrate the possibilities of a new curriculum.

"You shouldn't even have to say it," the teacher noted pointedly.

"Say what?" his colleague inquired.

"Say that they're not all like that. Of course they're not all like that. A few teenagers doing whatever do not represent the mass of adolescents. Right?"

The second teacher was viewing a thought marching before his mental eyes. Then, "Oh, sure. I was thinking. You know, Bill, we ought to teach statistics in high school."

"Yes. Certainly," came Bill's sardonic reply. "We have enough trouble teaching the math we do. I can just see the kids' averages plummet as we add another complex subject. The print media could have some new headlines and TV could present new specials on student failures."

Tom, his co-worker, was still manipulating invisible concepts as he half thought, half conversed. "Look," he said to gain Bill's attention. "I'm talking about understanding minimal statistical calculations. Let's say . . ."

Bill interrupts with a new pun being formulated. "Okay. Most people who have even heard of some statistical terms think an f score is a sexual tally." He laughed at his own wit. Then he continued on a more serious note. "We could teach the conceptual aspects of statistics."

"Something like that," Tom added. "We could teach the commonly used terms, their interpretation, and, I must stress, their limitations. With the exception of some kids who might be ready for it, we could omit the mathematical calculations involved."

"Applied statistics," Bill ventured.

"Right," Tom continued. "If the vast majority of people understand basic statistical concepts, the efforts of demagogues and hate mongers would be diffused. They wouldn't get away with half-truths and distortions. Stereotypical thinking would, to a great extent, fade away."

"You think it would be useful? Statistics without the calculations?" Bill asked somewhat dubious.

"Sure," Tom answered, pursuing the subject with more enthusiasm than when he had started. "Look. How do astronomers calculate the distance to stars and galaxies? They measure the difference between the real magnitude and the apparent magnitude. Right?"

"Yes," said Bill, not certain that he was comfortable with Tom's explanation. Something was missing.

Tom was. "I can't do the mathematics involved but I know enough to know it can be done. I know astronomers have some basis for their figures. People ought to have a general idea of what statistics can and can't do."

Bill jumped in. "If some guy or even a group commits a crime, people with statistical training would understand that the criminals might be from a particular ethnic group but that they don't represent that group." Bill stopped momentarily and continued as if lecturing a class.

"To be representative of a mass of people, the subjects would have to be randomly selected. In that way, all segments of the population in question would be represented more or less according to their numbers. But in the example I used, the criminals are only one element of the mass. They might be only one element out of a thousand. They represent themselves and only themselves."

"We agree," Tom nodded as he spoke. "An errant group of teenagers represents only a small group, not all the teenagers. To know what adolescents are really like, you'd have to get a scientific sampling, in reasonable numbers, of the whole adolescent population."

"Then, as I stated, when you're talking about some obnoxious teenager, you don't have to explain that 'They're not all like that.' " Bill started to rise.

Tom kept talking. "Everyone can understand a bell-shaped curve without the mathematics . . ."

"Time to go," Bill interjected.

Tom continued. "Should we talk to Mr. Berringer about developing a program in statistical fundamentals?"

"No," said Bill, moving toward the door. "The last thing the principal wants is another course to add to the curriculum. He keeps saying schools are pressured to add subjects but are never allowed to drop any to make room. If they do, they get criticized for not teaching the ones they dropped. Coming?"

PARENT: You're simply saying it's time to modernize the curriculum. Wouldn't the costs be staggering?

WRITER: I think there are more funds currently budgeted than are needed for a thorough overhaul. But as Rudyard Kipling once said, "That is another story."

Index